# EASY LOW CARB DIET SLOW COOKER RECIPES:

Best Healthy Low Carb Crock Pot Recipe Cookbook for Your Perfect Everyday Diet! (low carb chicken soup, ribs, pork chops, beef and low carb cake recipes)

## Helena Walker

D1373146

**Legal & Disclaimer**

The information contained in this book and its contents is not designed to replace or take the place of any form of medical or professional advice; and is not meant to replace the need for independent medical, financial, legal, or other professional advice or services, as may be required. The content and information in this book have been provided for educational and entertainment purposes only.

The content and information contained in this book have been compiled from sources deemed reliable, and it is accurate to the best of the Author's knowledge, information, and belief. However, the Author cannot guarantee its accuracy and validity and cannot be held liable for any errors and/or omissions. Further, changes are periodically made to this book as and when needed. Where appropriate and/or necessary, you must consult a professional (including but not limited to your doctor, attorney, financial advisor or such other professional advisor) before using any of the suggested remedies, techniques, or information in this book.

Upon using the contents and information contained in this book, you agree to hold harmless the Author from and against any damages, costs, and expenses, including any legal fees potentially resulting from the application of any of the information provided by this book. This disclaimer applies to any of the loss, damages or injury caused by the use and application, whether directly or indirectly, of any advice or information presented, whether for breach of contract, tort, negligence, personal injury, criminal intent, or under any other cause of action.

You agree to accept all risks of using the information presented in this book.

You agree that, by continuing to read this book, where appropriate and/or necessary, you shall consult a professional (including but not limited to your doctor, attorney, or financial advisor or such other advisor as needed) before using any of the suggested remedies, techniques, or information in this book.

# CONTENTS

## CONCLUSION

# INTRODUCTION

This book contains various types of delicious low-carb crock pot recipes. The crock pot is one type of slow cooker, which is a kind of stoneware pot surrounded by heating elements. The proven steps and strategies in this book will help you enter into a low-carb diet without compromising the taste and flavors of your food. This book contains 105 low-carb healthy and delicious recipes

Low-Carb Diet:

A low-carb diet limits your daily intake of carbohydrates and increases your portion of fats. This type of diet is also referred to as a low-carb, high-fat diet. Low-carb diets restrict the carbohydrates found in sugary foods, bread and pasta. It is high in fat and protein.

The concept of eating low-carb foods is quite simple. Carbohydrates and fats are the main sources of the energy needed by our bodies. Your body burns the carbs that you have consumed throughout the day and any excess carbs are stored in the form of fat. Storage of fat in the body leads you to gain weight. If you reduce the carb consumption, glycogen reserve levels fall and the body uses fats for energy instead of glycogen, derived from carbohydrates. Burning fat will help you lose weight. The process of burning fat for fuel is called lipolysis.

A low-carb diet is generally used for weight loss. Besides weight loss, the low-carb diet has various other health benefits, such as reducing the risk of the metabolic syndrome and type-2 diabetes. One study shows that adults with type-2 diabetes improved their blood sugar control while on a low-carb diet.

# Low-Carb Foods

## Meats and eggs

All types of meat and eggs have zero carbs. Low-carb meat includes turkey, lamb, beef, venison, chicken, bacon, veal, bison, etc.

- **Beef:** Beef is the best source of vitamin B12 and iron with zero carbohydrates.
- **Lamb:** Grass-fed lamb contains many beneficial nutrients like zinc, iron, niacin and vitamin B12. Lamb is rich in Omega-3 fatty acid and conjugated linoleic acid which has anticancer and antidiabetes properties.
- **Chicken:** Chicken is an excellent source of protein and other nutrients. It contains zero carbs.
- **Bacon:** Bacon is another popular type of meat for low-carb dieters. Bacon is a processed meat so try it moderate the amount while you are on a low-carb diet.
- **Eggs:** Eggs are the healthiest of foods and the best source of protein and other nutrients. One large egg contains six grams of protein and less than one gram of carbs. It is the ideal food for a low-carb diet.

## Vegetables

Most vegetables are low in carbs. Most of the carbs present in vegetables are in the form of fiber, which is not digested. Leafy green vegetables and cruciferous vegetables are low in carbs. Low-fat vegetables include tomatoes, onions, Brussels sprouts, broccoli, celery, kale, zucchini, cabbage, cauliflower, cucumbers, eggplant, spinach, Swiss chard, green beans, asparagus, mushrooms, etc.

- **Onions:** Onions are one of the tastiest vegetables used all around the globe. They have antioxidants, anti-inflammatories, and high fiber. One hundred grams of onions contain 9.3 grams of carbs.
- **Broccoli:** Broccoli is one of the cruciferous vegetables and contains vitamin K, vitamin C, and fiber. One hundred grams of broccoli contain 2.1 grams of carbs.
- **Brussels sprouts:** Brussels sprouts are one of the more nutritious vegetables and contain vitamin K and vitamin C, as well as various beneficial plant compounds. One hundred grams of Brussels sprouts contains 3.3 grams of carbs.
- **Tomatoes:** Tomatoes are one of the smart choices when you are on a low-carb diet. Tomatoes are low in carbs and a good source of essential nutrients. One hundred grams of tomatoes contain 3.9 grams of carbs.
- **Kale:** Kale is rich in various nutrients such as vitamin A, vitamin C, vitamin K, vitamin B6, calcium, manganese, etc. One hundred grams of kale contain 7 grams of carbs.
- **Cauliflower:** Cauliflower can be used as a substitute for mashed potatoes and rice. It contains vitamin C, vitamin K, and folate, etc. One hundred grams of cauliflower contain 2.7 grams of carbs.
- **Green Beans:** Green beans are a legume but they eaten as a vegetable. Green beans are the best source of nutrients like protein, fiber, potassium, vitamin C, vitamin K, and magnesium. One hundred grans of green beans contain 7.9 grams of carbs.
- **Cucumber:** Cucumbers are a healthy vegetable containing valuable fiber to improve your digestive health. It has a mild flavor. One hundred grams of cucumber contain 1.5 grams of carbs.

- **Eggplant:** Eggplants are a nonstarchy, high-fiber vegetable containing vitamin K, anthocyanins and phytonutrients. They are also low in carbs. One hundred grams of eggplant contain 4.8 grams of carbs.
- **Asparagus:** Asparagus is very high in protein compared to other vegetables. It contains vitamin C, vitamin K, folate, and fiber. One hundred grams of Asparagus contain 1.8 grams of carbs.
- **Mushrooms:** Mushrooms are low in carbs and a healthful option for low-carb diets. They contain various B vitamins and minerals such as potassium, selenium, and copper.

## Seafood

Low-carb seafood includes shrimp, cod, lobster, haddock, halibut, tuna, catfish, sardine, salmon, trout, etc.

- **Salmon:** Salmon are rich in vitamin B, selenium, potassium, vitamin D3, and heart-healthy omega-3 fatty acid. Salmon are very low in carbs.
- **Sardines:** Sardines are one of the healthier and more nutritious foods. They help in maintaining healthy fat and protein levels in your body.
- **Trout:** Trout is a fatty fish loaded with omega-3 fatty acid, and they also provide essential nutrients.

## Fruits

Low-carb fruits include avocado, kiwi, orange, lemon, raspberries, apricot, grape, strawberries, olives, etc.

- **Avocado:** Avocado is high in fiber and potassium. Most of the carbs in avocado are in the form of fiber. Therefore it contains no digestible carbs. One hundred grams of avocado contain 1.8 grams of carbs.

- **Apricot:** Apricot is one of the best sources of vitamin C and potassium. One hundred grams of apricot contain 11 grams of the carbs.
- **Strawberries:** Strawberries are a low-carb fruit enriched with manganese, vitamin C and antioxidants. One hundred grams of strawberries contain 7.7 grams of carbs.
- **Olives:** Olives are high in fat and rich in vitamin E, iron and copper. One hundred grams of olives contain 6.3 grams of carbs.

**Seeds and Nuts**

Seeds and nuts are low in carbs and high in fiber, fat, protein and micronutrients. Seeds and nuts include peanut, walnut, almonds, coconut, cashew, pistachios, sunflower seeds, chia seeds, flax seeds, hazelnuts, pumpkin seeds, etc.

- **Peanuts:** Peanuts (actually a legume) are an excellent source of vitamins and minerals. They contain vitamin E, magnesium and are high in fiber. One hundred grams of peanuts contain 16.1 grams of carbs.
- **Walnuts:** Walnuts are high in omega-3 fatty acid and alpha-lipoic acid. One hundred grams of walnuts contain 14 grams of carbs.
- **Hazelnuts:** Hazelnuts are naturally low in carbs. It is the perfect choice for low-carb diet plans. One hundred grams of hazelnuts contain 8 grams of carbs.

**Oils and Fats**

Healthy oils and fats include coconut oil, avocado oil, tallow, lard, extra-virgin olive oil, grass-fed butter, etc.

- **Extra-virgin olive oil:** Extra-virgin olive oil is a healthy fat containing anti-oxidants and anti-inflammatory compounds to keep your heart healthy.

- **Grass-fed Butter:** Butter from grass-feed cows is one of the healthiest choices for low-carb diets. It contains zero sugar and zero carbs.
- **Avocado oil:** Avocado oil is a rich source of oleic acid, which is very beneficial for the cardiovascular system and heart health.

## Dairy Products

Always choose dairy products without added sugar in a low-carb diet. Full-fat dairy products are a better choice for a low-carb diet.

- **Full Cream:** Full cream is the best alternative to milk for people on a low-carb diet. One hundred grams of full cream contain 4 grams of carbs.
- **Greek yogurt:** Compare to regular yogurt Greek yogurt is very thick and high in protein and various beneficial nutrients. One hundred grams of Greek yogurt contain 4.7 grams of carbs.
- **Cheddar Cheese:** Cheese is low in carbs and highly nutritious. It is one of the ingredients used in various types of recipes for enhanced taste. One hundred grams of cheddar cheese contain 1.4 grams of carbs.

## Beverages

Sugar-free beverages are allowed in a low-carb diet. Fruit juices, soft drinks, and beverages with added sugar should be avoided.

- **Green tea:** Green tea is beneficial for abdominal weight loss. It helps to reduce the metabolic syndrome with a low-carb diet.
- **Coffee:** Drinking coffee with two tablespoon of heavy cream and adding sugar-free sweetener is an ideal choice

for low-carb diet followers. Coffee is the biggest source of dietary antioxidants.

- **Soda:** Soda water (also known as club soda and seltzer water) is carbonated water, which is acceptable in low-carb diets only when it is sugar-free.

# FOOD TO AVOID OR LIMIT

- Processed snacks like chips, cookies, and crackers
- Bread
- Pasta
- Milk
- Rice
- Grains like quinoa, bulgur, and farro
- Oatmeal
- Lentils and Beans
- Sugar-rich food like candy, ice cream, cake and soda
- Starchy vegetables such as potatoes and sweet potatoes.
- High-carb fruits like bananas and grapes

# THE CROCK POT IS THE BEST APPLIANCE TO USE FOR LOW-CARB MEALS:

The crock pot is also known as a slow cooker. It is a handy appliances in which you can cook your meal at low temperature. Slow cooking prevents the food from burning, even foods cooked for long periods of time. Slow cooking also preserves the essential nutrients. When food is cooked at high temperatures the essential nutrients are lost. A slow cooker is a better choice for cooking beef brisket, chicken thighs, lamb shoulders, and pork shoulders. It tenderizes the meat. Slow cooking brings out the flavor of the food. Wide verities of food can be cooked in a slow cooker.

Slow cooking is especially beneficial for those people who follow a low-carb lifestyle. Preparing a meal at the end of the workday is very challenging for working people. The slow cooker/crock pot offers an ideal solution for them. Start your meal in the morning, put it into a slow cooker, set the time, and that's it. When you come home your healthy, delicious low-carb meal is ready to eat.

# BREAKFAST RECIPES

## 1-DELICIOUS BREAKFAST QUICHE

**Preparation Time: 10 minutes**

**Cooking Time: 3 hours 30 minutes**

**Serves: 6**

**Ingredients:**

- 5 eggs, lightly beaten
- 1/8 tsp nutmeg
- 1 cup green onions, sliced
- 1 cup cheddar cheese, grated
- 2 cups broccoli florets
- Pepper
- Salt

**Directions:**

- Spray the inside of a crock pot with cooking spray.
- In a mixing bowl, beat eggs with pepper, nutmeg, and salt.

- Add cheese and broccoli to the egg mixture and stir well.
- Pour egg mixture into the crock pot.
- Cover and cook on high for 3 hours.
- Add green onions to the top of the quiche, cover and cook on low for 30 minutes longer.
- Serve and enjoy.

**Nutritional Value (Amount per Serving):**

- Calories 144
- Fat 10 g
- Carbohydrates 3.8 g
- Sugar 1.3 g
- Protein 10.5 g
- Cholesterol 156 mg

# 2-Egg Sausage Breakfast Casserole

**Preparation Time: 10 minutes**

**Cooking Time: 4 hours**

**Serves: 8**

**Ingredients:**

- 10 eggs
- 3 garlic cloves, minced
- 3/4 cup whipping cream
- 1 cup cheddar cheese, shredded
- 12 oz sausage, cooked and sliced
- 2 cups broccoli, chopped
- 1/4 tsp pepper
- 1/2 tsp salt

**Directions:**

- Spray the inside of a crock pot with cooking spray.
- Layer half the sausage, half the broccoli, and half the shredded cheese in a crock pot.
- Repeat with remaining sausage, broccoli, and cheese.

- In a mixing bowl, whisk eggs, garlic, whipping cream, pepper, and salt until combined.
- Pour egg mixture over layered mixture.
- Cover and cook on low for 4 hours or until center is set.
- Serve and enjoy.

**Nutritional Value (Amount per Serving):**

- Calories 322
- Fat 25.8 g
- Carbohydrates 2.9 g
- Sugar 0.9 g
- Protein 19.7 g
- Cholesterol 268 mg

# 3-SPINACH FRITTATA

**Preparation Time: 10 minutes**

**Cooking Time: 1 hour 30 minutes**

**Serves: 6**

**Ingredients:**

- 3 eggs
- 3 extra egg whites
- 1 tomato, diced
- 1 cup spinach, chopped
- 2 Tbsp almond milk
- 1 cup mozzarella cheese, shredded
- 1 garlic clove, minced
- 1/2 cup onion, diced
- 1 Tbsp olive oil
- 1/4 tsp pepper
- Salt

**Directions:**

- Heat the oil in a pan over medium heat.

- Add onion to the pan and sauté for 4–5 minutes.
- Spray a crock pot inside with cooking spray.
- In a bowl, whisk together the sautéed onion, 3/4 cup mozzarella cheese, and remaining ingredients and pour into the crock pot.
- Top with remaining cheese. Cover and cook on low for 1 hour 30 minutes or until eggs are set.
- Serve and enjoy.

**Nutritional Value (Amount per Serving):**

- Calories 93
- Fat 6.6 g
- Carbohydrates 2.4 g
- Sugar 1.2 g
- Protein 6.4 g
- Cholesterol 84 mg

# 4-HEALTHY ARTICHOKE FRITTATA

**Preparation Time: 10 minutes**

**Cooking Time: 2 hours 5 minutes**

**Serves: 4**

**Ingredients:**

- 6 large eggs, lightly beaten
- 1/4 cup cheddar cheese, grated
- 1/4 cup green onion, chopped
- 1/4 cup bell pepper, chopped
- 1/2 tomato, chopped
- 3/4 cup artichoke hearts, chopped
- Pepper
- Salt

**Directions:**

- Spray a crock pot inside with cooking spray.
- In a bowl, whisk together eggs and vegetables and pour into the crock pot.
- Cover and cook on low for 2 hours or until eggs are set.

- Sprinkle grated cheese on top. Cover crock pot with the lid for 5 minutes or until cheese is melted.
- Slice and serve.

**Nutritional Value (Amount per Serving):**

- Calories 153
- Fat 9.9 g
- Carbohydrates 4.5 g
- Sugar 1.6 g
- Protein 12.3 g
- Cholesterol 286 mg

# 5-Vegetable Pesto Frittata

**Preparation Time: 10 minutes**

**Cooking Time: 3 hours**

**Serves: 4**

**Ingredients:**

- 10 eggs
- 2 Tbsp commercial pesto
- 2 Tbsp fresh basil, chopped
- 2 cups kale, chopped
- 1/2 cup fennel, chopped
- 1 cup red pepper, chopped
- 1 cup broccoli, chopped
- 1 cup zucchini, shredded
- 1/4 tsp red pepper flakes
- 1 tsp dried oregano
- 1 tsp garlic powder
- 1/2 cup feta cheese
- 1/4 cup coconut milk
- 1/2 tsp black pepper

- 1/2 tsp salt

**Directions:**

- In a large mixing bowl, whisk eggs, feta cheese, coconut milk, and spices.
- Spray a crock pot inside with cooking spray.
- Pour egg mixture into the crock pot.
- Add chopped vegetables and stir to combine. Sprinkle with fresh herbs.
- Top with pesto. Cover and cook on low for 3 hours or until eggs are set.
- Serve and enjoy.

**Nutritional Value (Amount per Serving):**

- Calories 321
- Fat 22.1 g
- Carbohydrates 13 g
- Sugar 5.2 g
- Protein 20.2 g
- Cholesterol 428 mg

# 6-Creamy Green Bean Casserole

**Preparation Time: 10 minutes**

**Cooking Time: 2 hours 30 minutes**

**Serves: 10**

**Ingredients:**

- 2 lb green beans, trimmed and cut into 1-inch pieces
- 1 Tbsp Dijon mustard
- 8 oz can water chestnuts, drained and sliced
- 1 cup leeks, sliced
- 1/4 cup coconut milk
- 10.5 oz can cream of mushroom soup
- 1 1/2 cups gouda cheese, shredded

**Directions:**

- In a crock pot stir together green beans, mustard, chestnuts, leeks, coconut milk, and cheddar cheese.
- Cover and cook on high for 2 1/2 hours.
- Serve and enjoy.

**Nutritional Value (Amount per Serving):**

- Calories 138

- Fat 7.8 g
- Carbohydrates 12 g
- Sugar 2.6 g
- Protein 6.6 g
- Cholesterol 19 mg

# 7-Healthy Vegetable Omelet

**Preparation Time: 10 minutes**

**Cooking Time: 1 hour 30 minutes**

**Serves: 4**

**Ingredients:**

- 6 eggs
- 1/2 cup onion, sliced
- 1 cup spinach
- 1/2 cup unsweetened almond milk
- 1 tsp parsley, dried
- 1 tsp garlic powder
- 1 bell pepper, diced
- 4 additional egg whites
- Pepper
- Salt

**Directions:**

- Spray a crock pot inside with cooking spray.

- In a large bowl, whisk together egg whites, eggs, parsley, garlic powder, almond milk, pepper, and salt.
- Stir in bell peppers, spinach, and onion.
- Pour egg mixture into the crock pot.
- Cover and cook on high for 1 1/2 hours or until eggs are set.
- Slice and serve.

**Nutritional Value (Amount per Serving):**

- Calories 200
- Fat 13.9 g
- Carbohydrates 6.8 g
- Sugar 4.1 g
- Protein 13.4 g
- Cholesterol 246 mg

# 8-Ham and Cheese Breakfast Omelet

**Preparation Time: 10 minutes**

**Cooking Time: 2 hours 30 minutes**

**Serves: 4**

**Ingredients:**

- 6 eggs
- 1 small onion, chopped
- 1 red bell pepper, sliced
- 1 garlic clove, minced
- 1 cup mozzarella cheese, shredded
- 3/4 cup ham, chopped
- 1/2 cup unsweetened almond milk
- Pepper
- Salt

**Directions:**

- Spray a crock pot inside with cooking spray.
- In a large bowl, whisk together eggs, garlic, pepper, salt, and milk.
- Pour egg mixture into the crock pot.

- Add ham, onions, and bell peppers to the crock pot.
- Cover and cook on high for 2 1/2 hours.
- Top with cheese, cover and cook until cheese is melted.
- Serve and enjoy.

**Nutritional Value (Amount per Serving):**

- Calories 242
- Fat 17.2 g
- Carbohydrates 7.5 g
- Sugar 2.8 g
- Protein 15.7 g
- Cholesterol 264 mg

# 9- SAUSAGE STUFFED BELL PEPPERS

**Preparation Time: 10 minutes**

**Cooking Time: 4 hours 10 minutes**

**Serves: 4**

**Ingredients:**

- 6 large eggs
- 1/2 lb ground breakfast sausage
- 4 bell peppers, tops cut off and seeded
- 4 oz green chilies, chopped
- 4 oz Jack cheese, shredded
- 1/8 tsp black pepper
- 1/4 tsp salt

**Directions:**

- Brown sausage in a pan over medium-high heat and drain excess oil.
- Pour 1/2 cup water into a crock pot.
- In a bowl, whisk eggs until smooth.
- Stir green chilies, cheese, black pepper, and salt into the eggs.

- Spoon egg mixture and brown sausage into each bell pepper.
- Place the stuffed bell peppers into the crock pot. Cover and cook for 4 hours.
- Serve and enjoy.

**Nutritional Value (Amount per Serving):**

- Calories 354
- Fat 21.9 g
- Carbohydrates 12 g
- Sugar 12 g
- Protein 26.7 g
- Cholesterol 348 mg

# 10-Creamy Cauliflower Mash

**Preparation Time: 10 minutes**

**Cooking Time: 6 hours**

**Serves: 4**

**Ingredients:**

- 1 medium cauliflower head, cut into florets
- 3 garlic cloves, minced
- 1 1/2 cups vegetable stock
- Pepper
- Salt

**Directions:**

- Add cauliflower florets, garlic, and stock to a crock pot.
- Cover and cook on low for 6 hours.
- Drain cauliflower well and transfer into a large bowl.
- Mash cauliflower using a potato masher until smooth and creamy.
- Season with pepper and salt.
- Stir well and serve.

**Nutritional Value (Amount per Serving):**

- Calories 38
- Fat 0.2 g
- Carbohydrates 8.1 g
- Sugar 3.5 g
- Protein 3 g
- Cholesterol 0 mg

# 11-Arugula Herb Frittata

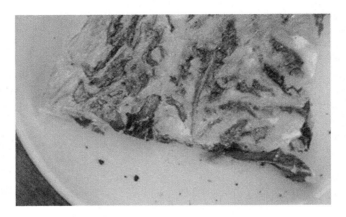

**Preparation Time: 10 minutes**

**Cooking Time: 3 hours**

**Serves: 6**

**Ingredients:**

- 8 eggs
- 1 1/2 cups red peppers, roasted and chopped
- 4 cups baby arugula
- 1 tsp oregano, dried
- 3/4 cup goat cheese, crumbled
- 1/2 cup onion, sliced
- 1/3 cup unsweetened almond milk
- Pepper
- Salt

**Directions:**

- Spray a crock pot inside with cooking spray.
- In a mixing bowl, whisk together eggs, oregano, and almond milk.
- Season with pepper and salt.

- Arrange red peppers, onion, arugula, and cheese in the crock pot.
- Pour egg mixture into the crock pot over the vegetables.
- Cover and cook on low for 3 hours.
- Serve and enjoy.

**Nutritional Value (Amount per Serving):**

- Calories 178
- Fat 12.8 g
- Carbohydrates 6 g
- Sugar 3.6 g
- Protein 11.4 g
- Cholesterol 233 mg

# 12-ITALIAN FRITTATA

**Preparation Time: 10 minutes**

**Cooking Time: 4 hours**

**Serves: 4**

**Ingredients:**

- 6 eggs
- 1/4 cup cherry tomatoes, sliced
- 4 oz mushrooms, sliced
- 2 tsp Italian seasoning
- 1/2 cup cheddar cheese, shredded
- Pepper
- Salt

**Directions:**

- Spray a crock pot inside with cooking spray.
- Spray a pan with cooking spray and heat over medium heat.
- Add mushrooms and cherry tomatoes to the pan and cook until softened.

- Transfer vegetables to the crock pot.
- In a bowl, whisk together eggs, cheese, pepper, and salt.
- Pour egg mixture in the crock pot.
- Cover and cook on low for 4 hours.
- Slice and serve.

**Nutritional Value (Amount per Serving):**

- Calories 167
- Fat 12 g
- Carbohydrates 2.3 g
- Sugar 1.6 g
- Protein 12.8 g
- Cholesterol 262 mg

# 13-Zucchini Bread

**Preparation Time: 10 minutes**

**Cooking Time: 3 hours**

**Serves: 12**

**Ingredients:**

- 3 eggs
- 1/2 tsp baking soda
- 1 1/2 tsp baking powder
- 2 tsp cinnamon
- 1/2 cup walnuts, chopped
- 2 cups zucchini, shredded
- 2 tsp vanilla
- 1/2 cup Pyure all purpose sweetener
- 1/3 cup coconut oil, softened
- 1/3 cup coconut flour
- 1 cup almond flour
- 1/2 tsp salt

**Directions:**

- In a bowl combine almond flour, baking soda, baking powder, cinnamon, coconut flour, and salt. Set aside.
- In another bowl, whisk together eggs, vanilla, sweetener, and oil.
- Add dry mixture to the wet mixture and fold well.
- Add walnuts and zucchini and fold well.
- Pour batter into a bread loaf pan.
- Place bread pan into the crock pot on a rack.
- Cover and cook on high for 3 hours.
- Cut bread loaf into slices and serve.

**Nutritional Value (Amount per Serving):**

- Calories 174
- Fat 15.4 g
- Carbohydrates 5.8 g
- Sugar 1.1 g
- Protein 5.3 g
- Cholesterol 41 mg

# 14-Cauliflower Casserole

**Preparation Time: 10 minutes**

**Cooking Time: 6 hours**

**Serves: 8**

**Ingredients:**

- 12 eggs
- 1/2 cup unsweetened almond milk
- 1 lb sausage, cooked and crumbled
- 1 cauliflower head, shredded
- 2 cups cheddar cheese, shredded
- Pepper
- Salt

**Directions:**

- Spray a crock pot inside with cooking spray.
- In a bowl, whisk together eggs, almond milk, pepper, and salt.
- Add about a third of the shredded cauliflower into the bottom of the crock pot. Season with pepper and salt.

- Top with about a third of the sausage and a third of the cheese.
- Repeat the same layers 2 more times.
- Pour egg mixture into the crock pot.
- Cover and cook on low for 6 hours.
- Serve and enjoy.

**Nutritional Value (Amount per Serving):**

- Calories 443
- Fat 35.6 g
- Carbohydrates 3.5 g
- Sugar 2 g
- Protein 27.4 g
- Cholesterol 323 mg

# 15-LEMON CINNAMON APPLES

**Preparation Time: 10 minutes**

**Cooking Time: 3 hours**

**Serves: 10**

**Ingredients:**

- 9 cups apple, peeled, cored, diced
- 2 Tbsp fresh lemon juice
- 1/2 tsp nutmeg
- 2 tsp ground cinnamon
- 1 1/2 cups water

**Directions:**

- Add all ingredients to a crock pot and stir well.
- Cover and cook on high for 3 hours.
- Stir well and serve.

**Nutritional Value (Amount per Serving):**

- Calories 50
- Fat 0.2 g
- Carbohydrates 13.1 g

- Sugar 10.1 g
- Protein 0.3 g
- Cholesterol 0 mg

# POULTRY RECIPES

## 16-Easy Mexican Chicken

**Preparation Time: 10 minutes**

**Cooking Time: 5 hours**

**Serves: 4**

**Ingredients:**

- 8 chicken thighs, bone- in and skin-on
- 1/4 tsp red pepper flakes
- 1/4 cup green onion, sliced
- 1 packet taco seasoning
- 1 cup chicken stock

**Directions:**

- Add stock and half the taco seasoning to a crock pot. Stir well to blend.
- Place chicken thighs in the crock pot and sprinkle remaining seasoning on top of chicken.

- Cover and cook on low for 5 hours.
- Garnish with red pepper flakes and green onions.
- Serve and enjoy.

**Nutritional Value (Amount per Serving):**

- Calories 565
- Fat 21.8 g
- Carbohydrates 1.7 g
- Sugar 0.6 g
- Protein 84.8 g
- Cholesterol 260 mg

# 17-SUPER DELICIOUS RANCH CHICKEN

**Preparation Time: 10 minutes**

**Cooking Time: 6 hours**

**Serves: 6**

**Ingredients:**

- 2 lb chicken breasts, boneless
- 1 packet ranch dressing mix
- 4 oz cream cheese
- 3 Tbsp butter

**Directions:**

- Place chicken in a crock pot.
- Add cream cheese and butter on top of the chicken. Sprinkle ranch dressing on top of the chicken.
- Cover and cook on low for 6 hours.
- Shred the chicken using forks and serve.

**Nutritional Value (Amount per Serving):**

- Calories 404
- Fat 23.6 g

- Carbohydrates 0.5 g
- Sugar 0 g
- Protein 45.2 g
- Cholesterol 171 mg

# 18-Balsamic Chicken

**Preparation Time: 10 minutes**

**Cooking Time: 3 hours**

**Serves: 8**

**Ingredients:**

- 3 lb chicken breasts, sliced in half
- 3/4 cup balsamic vinegar
- 2 tsp dried onion, minced
- 2 tsp dried basil
- 3 garlic cloves, minced
- 1 Tbsp olive oil
- 1/4 tsp pepper
- 1/2 tsp salt

**Directions:**

- Add garlic and olive oil to a crock pot.
- In a small bowl, mix together the dry seasonings.
- Rub chicken breasts with the seasonings and place them in the crock pot.
- Pour balsamic vinegar over chicken breasts.
- Cover and cook on low for 3 hours.

- Slice and serve.

**Nutritional Value (Amount per Serving):**

- Calories 345
- Fat 14.4 g
- Carbohydrates 0.7 g
- Sugar 0.1 g
- Protein 49.3 g
- Cholesterol 151 mg

# 19-Parmesan Chicken Wings

**Preparation Time: 10 minutes**

**Cooking Time: 3 hours 10 minutes**

**Serves: 8**

**Ingredients:**

- 4 lb chicken wings
- 1 cup Parmesan cheese, shredded
- 5 garlic cloves, minced
- 1/2 cup butter, melted
- 1/4 tsp pepper
- 1 tsp salt

**Directions:**

- Place chicken wings in a crock pot and season with pepper and salt.
- In a small bowl, mix together garlic and butter.
- Pour garlic butter mixture over the chicken wings and stir well to coat.

- Cover and cook on high for 3 hours.
- Arrange chicken wings on a baking tray and broil for 5 minutes on each side.
- Remove chicken wings from oven and top with shredded cheese.
- Return chicken wings to the oven for 1–2 minutes until the cheese has melted.
- Serve and enjoy.

**Nutritional Value (Amount per Serving):**

- Calories 577
- Fat 31.1 g
- Carbohydrates 1 g
- Sugar 0 g
- Protein 69.7 g
- Cholesterol 240 mg

# 20-Delicious Creamy Chicken

**Preparation Time: 10 minutes**

**Cooking Time: 6 hours**

**Serves: 6**

**Ingredients:**

- 2 lb chicken breasts, skinless and boneless, cut into 6 pieces.
- 3 Tbsp Parmesan cheese, grated
- 4 oz cream cheese, cut in pieces
- 1/4 cup bell pepper, diced
- 1/2 cup chicken stock
- 1 packet dry ranch seasoning mix
- 1 can (10.5 oz) cream of chicken soup

**Directions:**

- Mix ranch seasoning and cream of chicken soup in a crock pot.
- Slowly add stock and stir well.
- Add bell pepper and stir well.

- Add chicken and stir well. Cover and cook on low for 6 hours.
- About a half hour before cooking time is up add the parmesan cheese and the cream cheese.
- Cover and continue cooking for 30 minutes.
- Stir well and serve.

**Nutritional Value (Amount per Serving):**

- Calories 420
- Fat 21.8 g
- Carbohydrates 4.5 g
- Sugar 0.6 g
- Protein 48 g
- Cholesterol 163 mg

# 21-MUSTARD CHICKEN

**Preparation Time: 10 minutes**

**Cooking Time: 8 hours**

**Serves: 4**

**Ingredients:**

- 4 chicken thighs
- 2 Tbsp olive oil
- 1/4 cup Dijon mustard
- 2 Tbsp honey
- 1 tsp fresh rosemary, chopped
- 1/4 tsp pepper
- 1/2 tsp sea salt

**Directions:**

- Place chicken in a crock pot.
- In a small bowl, mix together oil, mustard, honey, pepper, rosemary, and salt. Pour over chicken.
- Cover and cook on low for 8 hours.

- Serve and enjoy.

**Nutritional Value (Amount per Serving):**

- Calories 381
- Fat 18.5 g
- Carbohydrates 9.8 g
- Sugar 8.8 g
- Protein 43 g
- Cholesterol 130 mg

# 22-Chicken Tomatillo Drumsticks

**Preparation Time: 10 minutes**

**Cooking Time: 6 hours**

**Serves: 4**

**Ingredients:**

- 4 chicken drumsticks, bone-in, and skin removed
- 1 Tbsp apple cider vinegar
- 1 cup tomatillo salsa
- 1 tsp olive oil
- 1 tsp dried oregano
- Pepper
- Salt

**Directions:**

- Add all ingredients to a crock pot and stir well to combine.
- Cover and cook on low for 6 hours.
- Serve and enjoy.

**Nutritional Value (Amount per Serving):**

- Calories 100
- Fat 4.2 g
- Carbohydrates 2.2 g
- Sugar 0 g
- Protein 13 g
- Cholesterol 40 mg

# 23-Juicy Shredded Turkey

**Preparation Time: 10 minutes**

**Cooking Time: 8 hours**

**Serves: 10**

**Ingredients:**

- 4 lb turkey breast, skinless, boneless, and halved
- 12 oz chicken stock
- 1 packet onion soup mix
- 1/2 cup butter, cubed

**Directions:**

- Place turkey in a crock pot.
- Combine together butter, chicken stock, and onion soup mix and pour over the turkey.
- Cover and cook on low for 8 hours.
- Shred turkey using forks and serve.

**Nutritional Value (Amount per Serving):**

- Calories 274
- Fat 12.3 g
- Carbohydrates 8.2 g
- Sugar 6.5 g
- Protein 31.2 g
- Cholesterol 102 mg

# 24-TENDER AND MOIST TURKEY BREAST

**Preparation Time: 10 minutes**

**Cooking Time: 4 hours**

**Serves: 12**

**Ingredients:**

- 6 lb turkey breast, bone-in
- 3 fresh rosemary sprigs
- 1/2 cup chicken stock
- 3 garlic cloves, peeled
- Pepper
- Salt

**Directions:**

- Place turkey breast in a crock pot.
- Add stock, garlic, and rosemary on top. Season with pepper and salt.
- Cover and cook on low for 4 hours or until meat is tender.
- Serve and enjoy.

**Nutritional Value (Amount per Serving):**

- Calories 237
- Fat 3.8 g
- Carbohydrates 9.9 g
- Sugar 8 g
- Protein 38.8 g
- Cholesterol 98 mg

# 25-PESTO CHICKEN

**Preparation Time: 10 minutes**

**Cooking Time: 7 hours**

**Serves: 4**

**Ingredients:**

- 4 chicken breasts, skinless and boneless
- 3 garlic cloves, minced
- 1/2 small onion, diced
- 1 cup frozen spinach, thawed and drained
- 1/2 cup Parmesan cheese, grated
- 2/3 cup commercial pesto
- 2 Tbsp chicken stock
- Pepper
- Salt

**Directions:**

- Place the chicken in a crock pot and season with pepper and salt.

- In a bowl, combine the chicken stock, pesto, onion, and spinach.
- Pour bowl mixture over the chicken.
- Cover and cook on low for 7 hours.
- Top with Parmesan cheese. Cover for 5 minutes and cook until the cheese has melted.
- Serve and enjoy.

**Nutritional Value (Amount per Serving):**

- Calories 541
- Fat 32.7 g
- Carbohydrates 4.5 g
- Sugar 3.1 g
- Protein 52.7 g
- Cholesterol 155 mg

# 26-Balsamic Chicken

**Preparation Time: 10 minutes**

**Cooking Time: 4 hours**

**Serves: 10**

**Ingredients:**

- 6 chicken breasts, skinless and boneless
- 1/2 tsp thyme
- 1 tsp dried oregano
- 1/2 cup balsamic vinegar
- 3 garlic cloves
- 1 onion, sliced
- 1 tsp dried basil
- 1 tsp dried rosemary
- 1 Tbsp olive oil
- 14 oz can tomatoes, diced
- Pepper
- Salt

## Directions:

- Add all ingredients to a crock pot and stir well.
- Cover and cook on high for 4 hours.
- Stir well and serve.

## Nutritional Value (Amount per Serving):

- Calories 197
- Fat 8 g
- Carbohydrates 3.8 g
- Sugar 1.9 g
- Protein 25.9 g
- Cholesterol 78 mg

# 27-Mexican Salsa Chicken

**Preparation Time: 10 minutes**

**Cooking Time: 8 hours**

**Serves: 8**

**Ingredients:**

- 3 1/2 lb chicken
- 1 tsp cumin
- 2 garlic cloves
- 1 cup onion, chopped
- 14 oz can tomatoes, diced
- 1 fresh lime juice
- 1 tsp oregano
- 1 can (4 oz)  chilies
- 1 tsp salt

**Directions:**

- Add all ingredients to a crock pot and stir well.
- Cover and cook on low for 8 hours.
- Remove chicken from the crock pot and place in a bowl.

- Shred the chicken using forks.
- Blend the mixture left in the crock pot using a blender or immersion blender until smooth.
- Return the shredded chicken to the crock pot and stir well. Cover and cook for 5 minutes longer.
- Serve and enjoy.

**Nutritional Value (Amount per Serving):**

- Calories 324
- Fat 6.2 g
- Carbohydrates 5.6 g
- Sugar 2.3 g
- Protein 58.4 g
- Cholesterol 153 mg

# 28-TURKEY WITH MUSHROOMS

**Preparation Time: 10 minutes**

**Cooking Time: 6 hours**

**Serves: 6**

**Ingredients:**

- 1 1/2 lb turkey breast cutlets
- 1 tsp sage, minced
- 8 oz mushrooms, sliced
- 1 medium onion, sliced
- 1/4 cup water
- 1 Tbsp butter
- 1/4 tsp pepper
- 1/8 Tsp salt

**Directions:**

- Heat butter in a pan over medium heat.

- Add mushrooms and onion to the pan and sauté until softened.
- Add half the mushroom and onion mixture to a crock pot.
- Add turkey to the crock pot and sprinkle with pepper, sage, and salt.
- Pour remaining mushroom and onion mixture over the turkey.
- Pour the water into the crock pot.
- Cover and cook on low for 6 hours.
- Serve and enjoy.

**Nutritional Value (Amount per Serving):**

- Calories 142
- Fat 1.2 g
- Carbohydrates 3.1 g
- Sugar 1.4 g
- Protein 29.5 g
- Cholesterol 47 mg

# 29-Curried Chicken Wings

**Preparation Time: 10 minutes**

**Cooking Time: 6 hours**

**Serves: 6**

**Ingredients:**

- 3 lb chicken wings
- 2 oz Thai basil, minced
- 8 oz green curry paste
- 1 Tbsp fresh cilantro, minced
- 1 Tbsp fresh ginger, minced
- 1 Tbsp coconut milk

**Directions:**

- Add chicken wings to a crock pot.
- In a bowl, whisk together coconut milk, cilantro, ginger, basil, and curry paste.
- Pour coconut milk mixture over the chicken wings and toss well.

- Cover and cook on low for 6 hours.
- Stir well and serve.

**Nutritional Value (Amount per Serving):**

- Calories 322
- Fat 14.3 g
- Carbohydrates 6.3 g
- Sugar 0.1 g
- Protein 39.6 g
- Cholesterol 121 mg

# 30-Bacon Herb Chicken

**Preparation Time: 10 minutes**

**Cooking Time: 8 hours**

**Serves: 4**

**Ingredients:**

- 5 chicken breasts, skinless and boneless
- 1 Tbsp oregano, dried
- 2 Tbsp thyme, dried
- 10 bacon slices, chopped
- 5 Tbsp olive oil
- 1 Tbsp rosemary, dried
- 1 Tbsp salt

**Directions:**

- Add all ingredients to a crock pot and mix well.
- Cover and cook on low for 8 hours.
- Shred the chicken using forks and serve.

**Nutritional Value (Amount per Serving):**

- Calories 619

- Fat 28.6 g
- Carbohydrates 2.1 g
- Sugar 0.1 g
- Protein 55.3 g
- Cholesterol 146 mg

# BEEF, PORK AND LAMB RECIPES

## 31-SIMPLE GARLIC PORK TENDERLOIN

**Preparation Time: 10 minutes**

**Cooking Time: 6 hours**

**Serves: 8**

**Ingredients:**

- 2 lb pork tenderloin
- 1/2 tsp red pepper flakes
- 1 Tbsp Worcestershire sauce
- 1/2 cup balsamic vinegar
- 3 garlic cloves, minced
- 1 1/2 Tbsp coconut aminos
- 1 Tbsp extra-virgin olive oil
- 1/2 tsp sea salt

## Directions:

- Place pork tenderloin in a crock pot.
- Drizzle olive oil over the pork tenderloin and sprinkle with garlic.
- In a small bowl, mix together remaining ingredients and pour over the pork tenderloin.
- Cover and cook on low for 6 hours.
- Serve and enjoy.

## Nutritional Value (Amount per Serving):

- Calories 184
- Fat 5.8 g
- Carbohydrates 1 g
- Sugar 0.5 g
- Protein 29.8 g
- Cholesterol 83 mg

# 32-Flavorful Lamb Rogan Josh

**Preparation Time: 15 minutes**

**Cooking Time: 6 hours 15 minutes**

**Serves: 6**

**Ingredients:**

- 2 lb leg of lamb, cubed
- 14 oz can tomatoes, crushed
- 1 Tbsp olive oil
- 1 tsp garam masala
- 1 tsp turmeric
- 1/2 tsp ground cloves
- 1 1/2 tsp ground cardamom
- 1 1/2 tsp ground cumin
- 1 Tbsp ground coriander
- 1 Tbsp tomato paste
- 1 tsp chili powder
- 2 tsp garlic, minced
- 1 Tbsp ginger, crushed
- 1 onion, diced

## Directions:

- Spray a pan with cooking spray and heat over high heat.
- Brown the meat in the hot pan. Remove meat from the pan and set aside.
- Heat oil in the same pan. Add onion, ginger, and garlic and sauté until onion is softened.
- Add chili powder, garam masala, turmeric, cloves, cardamom, cumin, coriander, and tomato paste to the pan and stir until fragrant.
- Transfer pan mixture to a crock pot along with the meat and crushed tomatoes, and stir well.
- Cover and cook on low for 6 hours.
- Serve and enjoy.

## Nutritional Value (Amount per Serving):

- Calories 316
- Fat 11.5 g
- Carbohydrates 7.7 g
- Sugar 3.5 g
- Protein 43.8 g
- Cholesterol 136 mg

# 33-DIJON LAMB CHOPS

**Preparation Time: 10 minutes**

**Cooking Time: 5 hours**

**Serves: 4**

**Ingredients:**

- 4 lean lamb chops
- 1/2 tsp paprika
- 1 Tbsp fresh rosemary, minced
- 1 1/2 tbsp mustard seeds
- 2 garlic cloves, minced
- 1/2 cup Dijon mustard
- 1/4 tsp pepper

**Directions:**

- In a small bowl, mix together Dijon mustard, pepper, rosemary, mustard seeds, and garlic.
- Coat lamb chops with the mustard mixture and place them in a crock pot.
- Cover and cook on low for 5 hours.
- Serve and enjoy.

**Nutritional Value (Amount per Serving):**

- Calories 230
- Fat 10.6 g
- Carbohydrates 4.4 g
- Sugar 0.6 g
- Protein 27.6 g
- Cholesterol 80 mg

# 34-Spinach Lamb Curry

**Preparation Time: 15 minutes**

**Cooking Time: 6 hours 5 minutes**

**Serves: 6**

**Ingredients:**

- 2 lb lamb stew meat
- 1/3 cup plain yogurt
- 4 cups spinach, chopped
- 2 cups chicken stock
- 1/4 tsp cinnamon
- 1/2 tsp paprika
- 1/2 tsp red pepper flakes
- 1/4 tsp turmeric
- 1/8 tsp ground cloves
- 2 tsp ground coriander
- 1 Tbsp ground cumin
- 1 Tbsp fresh ginger, grated
- 5 garlic cloves, minced
- 1 Tbsp olive oil

- 1 onion, diced
- 1 tsp salt

**Directions:**

- Heat oil in a pan over medium heat.
- Add onion and sauté for 4 minutes.
- Add ginger and garlic and sauté for 1–2 minutes.
- Transfer pan mixture to a crock pot.
- Add remaining ingredients to the crock pot except for the yogurt and spinach.
- Stir everything well. Cover and cook on low for 6 hours.
- Just before serving add the yogurt and spinach and stir until spinach is wilted.
- Serve and enjoy.

**Nutritional Value (Amount per Serving):**

- Calories 338
- Fat 14.2 g
- Carbohydrates 5.9 g
- Sugar 2.2 g
- Protein 44.7 g
- Cholesterol 137 mg

# 35-Perfect Shredded Pork

**Preparation Time: 10 minutes**

**Cooking Time: 8 hours**

**Serves: 12**

**Ingredients:**

- 4 lb pork shoulder
- 3/4 cup water
- 1/4 cup apple cider vinegar
- 1 tsp onion powder
- 1 tsp garlic powder
- 1 tsp cayenne pepper
- 1 tsp pepper
- 2 Tbsp paprika
- 1 tsp kosher salt

**Directions:**

- In a small bowl, mix together all dry spices and rub onto all sides of the meat.
- Add water and apple cider vinegar to a crock pot.

- Place meat in the crock pot.
- Cover and cook on low for 8 hours.
- Remove meat from the pot and shred using forks.
- Serve and enjoy.

**Nutritional Value (Amount per Serving):**

- Calories 448
- Fat 32.5 g
- Carbohydrates 1.2 g
- Sugar 0.3 g
- Protein 35.5 g
- Cholesterol 136 mg

# 36-Easy Ranch Pork Chops

**Preparation Time: 10 minutes**

**Cooking Time: 8 hours**

**Serves: 4**

**Ingredients:**

- 4 pork chops, boneless
- 3/4 cup chicken stock
- 10.5 oz can cream of chicken soup
- 4 oz cream cheese
- 1 packet ranch dressing mix

**Directions:**

- Place pork chops in a crock pot.
- Combine stock, cream of chicken soup, cream cheese, and ranch dressing mix and pour over the pork chops.
- Cover and cook on low for 8 hours.
- Serve and enjoy.

**Nutritional Value (Amount per Serving):**

- Calories 425
- Fat 34.2 g
- Carbohydrates 6.5 g
- Sugar 0.6 g
- Protein 22 g
- Cholesterol 106 mg

# 37-Tasty Pork Roast

**Preparation Time: 10 minutes**

**Cooking Time: 6 hours**

**Serves: 6**

**Ingredients:**

- 3 lb pork roast
- 2 tsp garlic, minced
- 2 Tbsp honey
- 2 Tbsp soy sauce
- 1/4 cup balsamic vinegar
- 1 cup chicken stock

**Directions:**

- Place pork roast in a crock pot.
- Combine the remaining ingredients and pour over the pork roast.
- Cover and cook on high for 6 hours.
- Remove meat from the crock pot and shred using forks.
- Pour crock pot liquid over shredded meat and serve.

**Nutritional Value (Amount per Serving):**

- Calories 499
- Fat 21.5 g
- Carbohydrates 6.7 g
- Sugar 6 g
- Protein 65.2 g
- Cholesterol 195 mg

# 38-TASTY AND SPICY BEEF CHILI

**Preparation Time: 10 minutes**

**Cooking Time: 10 hours**

**Serves: 4**

**Ingredients:**

- 1 lb lean beef, cubed
- 1/2 tsp white pepper
- 1/2 tsp black pepper
- 1/2 tsp oregano
- 1 Tbsp paprika
- 8 oz can tomato sauce
- 1/2 tsp ground chipotle
- 1/2 tsp cayenne pepper
- 2 Tbsp chili powder
- 1 Tbsp garlic powder
- 2 Tbsp onion powder

**Directions:**

- Heat a pan over medium-high heat.

- Place meat in the pan and sauté until brown. Drain the beef on paper towels to remove any excess grease.
- Place browned meat in a crock pot.
- Add remaining ingredients over the meat.
- Cover and cook on low for 10 hours.
- Serve and enjoy.

**Nutritional Value (Amount per Serving):**

- Calories 263
- Fat 8.2 g
- Carbohydrates 11 g
- Sugar 4.6 g
- Protein 36.7 g
- Cholesterol 101 mg

# 39-FLAVORFUL SHREDDED PORK

**Preparation Time: 10 minutes**

**Cooking Time: 8 hours**

**Serves: 10**

**Ingredients:**

- 3 lb pork shoulder roast, boneless and cut into 4 pieces
- 1/2 Tbsp cumin
- 1/2 Tbsp fresh oregano
- 2/3 cup orange juice
- 5 garlic cloves
- Pepper
- Salt

**Directions:**

- Add pork roast to a crock pot. Season with pepper and salt.
- Add garlic, cumin, oregano, and orange juice to a blender and blend until smooth.
- Pour blended mixture over the pork and stir well.
- Cover and cook on low for 8 hours.
- Remove pork from the crock pot and shred using forks.

- Return shredded pork to the crock pot and stir well.
- Serve warm and enjoy.

**Nutritional Value (Amount per Serving):**

- Calories 359
- Fat 27.8 g
- Carbohydrates 2.1 g
- Sugar 1.1 g
- Protein 23.2 g
- Cholesterol 96 mg

# 40-Steak Fajitas

**Preparation Time: 10 minutes**

**Cooking Time: 6 hours**

**Serves: 6**

**Ingredients:**

- 2 lb beef, sliced
- 1 1/2 Tbsp fajita seasoning
- 20 oz chunky salsa
- 1 bell pepper, sliced
- 1 onion, sliced

**Directions:**

- Add salsa to a crock pot.
- Add remaining ingredients to the crock pot and stir to mix.
- Cover the crock pot with its lid and cook on low for 6 hours.
- Stir well and serve.

**Nutritional Value (Amount per Serving):**

- Calories 333
- Fat 9.7 g
- Carbohydrates 11.9 g
- Sugar 5 g
- Protein 47.8 g
- Cholesterol 135 mg

# 41-Simple Seasoned Pork Chops

**Preparation Time: 10 minutes**

**Cooking Time: 6 hours**

**Serves: 4**

**Ingredients:**

- 4 pork chops
- 2 garlic cloves, minced
- 2 Tbsp butter, melted
- 3/4 tsp poultry seasoning
- 1 onion, chopped
- 1 1/2 cups chicken stock
- 1/2 tsp salt

**Directions:**

- In a large bowl, mix together butter, broth, poultry seasoning and salt.
- Pour the mixture into a crock pot.
- Add pork chops, onion, and garlic to the crock pot.

- Cover and cook on low for 6 hours.
- Serve and enjoy.

**Nutritional Value (Amount per Serving):**

- Calories 337
- Fat 26.2 g
- Carbohydrates 3.8 g
- Protein 20.3 g
- Sugar 1.5 g
- Cholesterol 84 mg

# 42-Spicy Beef Brisket

**Preparation Time: 10 minutes**

**Cooking Time: 7 hours**

**Serves: 6**

**Ingredients:**

- 3 lb beef brisket
- 1 Tbsp Worcestershire sauce
- 1 Tbsp chili powder
- 3 garlic cloves, chopped
- 1/2 onion, chopped
- 1 tsp cumin
- 3 Tbsp chili sauce
- 1/4 cup beef broth
- 1 1/2 tsp liquid smoke
- 1/2 tsp black pepper

**Directions:**

- In a small bowl, mix together chili powder, pepper, cumin, Worcestershire sauce, and garlic. Rub this mixture over the brisket.

- Place beef brisket in the crock pot.
- Mix together broth, chili sauce, onion, and liquid smoke and pour it over the brisket.
- Cover and cook on low for 7 hours.
- Remove brisket from the crock pot and cut into slices.
- Serve and enjoy.

**Nutritional Value (Amount per Serving):**

- Calories 439
- Fat 14.5 g
- Carbohydrates 3.1 g
- Sugar 1.1 g
- Protein 69.5 g
- Cholesterol 203 mg

# 43-Delicious Pork Carnitas

**Preparation Time: 10 minutes**

**Cooking Time: 6 hours**

**Serves: 6**

**Ingredients:**

- 2 lb pork tenderloin
- 1 jalapeño pepper, seeded, chopped
- 3 garlic cloves, minced
- 1/2 onion, chopped
- 1 Tbsp olive oil
- 1 orange juice
- 1 lime juice
- 2 tsp ground cumin
- 1 Tbsp oregano, dried

**Directions:**

- Combine olive oil, ground cumin, and oregano. Rub this well over the pork tenderloin.
- Place tenderloin in a crock pot.
- Top with remaining ingredients.

- Cover and cook on low for 6 hours.
- Remove meat from the crock pot and shred it using forks.
- Serve and enjoy.

**Nutritional Value (Amount per Serving):**

- Calories 256
- Fat 7.9 g
- Carbohydrates 4.4 g
- Sugar 1.9 g
- Protein 40.1 g
- Cholesterol 110 mg

# 44-Creamy Beef Stroganoff

**Preparation Time: 10 minutes**

**Cooking Time: 8 hours**

**Serves: 2**

**Ingredients:**

- 1/2 lb beef stew meat
- 1/2 cup sour cream
- 3 oz mushrooms, sliced
- 10 oz can cream of mushroom soup
- 1 onion, chopped
- Pepper
- salt

**Directions:**

- Add all ingredients except sour cream to a crock pot and mix well.
- Cover and cook on low for 8 hours.
- Add sour cream and stir well.
- Serve and enjoy.

**Nutritional Value (Amount per Serving):**

- Calories 425
- Fat 23.4 g
- Carbohydrates 13.7 g
- Sugar 4.2 g
- Protein 39.3 g
- Cholesterol 127 mg

# 45-TENDER BEEF CARNITAS

**Preparation Time: 10 minutes**

**Cooking Time: 8 hours**

**Serves: 4**

**Ingredients:**

- 2 lb flank steak
- 1 green bell pepper, chopped
- 1 onion, chopped
- 1 jalapeño, seeded and chopped
- 1 red bell pepper, chopped
- For the rub:
- 1/4 tsp cayenne pepper
- 1 tsp cumin
- 2 tsp chili powder
- 1/4 tsp garlic powder
- 1/4 tsp onion powder
- 1/2 tsp black pepper
- 1 tsp salt

## Directions:

- In a small bowl, mix together all spice ingredients and rub them over the flank steak.
- Place the flank steak in a crock pot.
- Add jalapeño pepper, bell peppers, and onion over the steak.
- Cover and cook on low for 8 hours.
- Remove meat from crock pot and shred using forks.
- Return shredded meat to the crock pot.
- Stir well and serve.

## Nutritional Value (Amount per Serving):

- Calories 476
- Fat 19.4 g
- Carbohydrates 7.8 g
- Sugar 4 g
- Protein 64.4 g
- Cholesterol 125 mg

# FISH and SEAFOOD RECIPES

## 46-Coconut Shrimp Curry

**Preparation Time: 10 minutes**

**Cooking Time: 2 hours 30 minutes**

**Serves: 4**

**Ingredients:**

- 1 lb shrimp
- 1/4 cup fresh cilantro, chopped
- 2 tsp lemon garlic seasoning
- 1 Tbsp curry paste
- 15 oz water
- 30 oz coconut milk

**Directions:**

- Add coconut milk, cilantro, lemon garlic seasoning, curry paste, and water to a crock pot and stir well.
- Cover and cook on high for 2 hours.

- Add shrimp, cover and cook for 30 minutes longer.
- Serve and enjoy.

**Nutritional Value (Amount per Serving):**

- Calories 200
- Fat 7.7 g
- Carbohydrates 4.6 g
- Sugar 0 g
- Protein 26 g
- Cholesterol 239 mg

# 47-Delicious Fish Curry

**Preparation Time: 10 minutes**

**Cooking Time: 2 hours**

**Serves: 4**

**Ingredients:**

- 1 lb cod fish fillets
- 12 oz carrots, cut into julienne strips
- 1 bell pepper, sliced
- 1 tsp garlic powder
- 1 tsp ground ginger
- 1 Tbsp curry powder
- 3 Tbsp red curry paste
- 15 oz coconut milk
- Pepper
- Salt

**Directions:**

- Add coconut milk to a crock pot and whisk in curry powder, garlic powder, ground ginger, and curry paste.

- Stir in carrots and bell peppers.
- Place cod fillets in the sauce.
- Cover and cook on low for 2 hours.
- Season with pepper and salt.
- Serve and enjoy.

**Nutritional Value (Amount per Serving):**

- Calories 232
- Fat 6.5 g
- Carbohydrates 14.1 g
- Sugar 5.2 g
- Protein 27.1 g
- Cholesterol 62 mg

# 48-Lemon Dill Salmon

**Preparation Time: 10 minutes**

**Cooking Time: 2 hours**

**Serves: 4**

**Ingredients:**

- 1 lb salmon fillet, skin-on
- 2 Tbsp fresh dill, chopped
- 1/2 lemon juice
- 1 1/2 cups vegetable stock
- 1 lemon, sliced
- Pepper
- Salt

**Directions:**

- Line a crock pot with parchment paper. Place lemon slices on the bottom of the crock pot and then place the salmon on top of the slices
- Season salmon with pepper and salt.
- Add lemon juice and stock to the crock pot.

- Cover and cook on low for 2 hours.
- Serve and enjoy.

**Nutritional Value (Amount per Serving):**

- Calories 162
- Fat 7.7 g
- Carbohydrates 2.9 g
- Sugar 1 g
- Protein 22.5 g
- Cholesterol 50 mg

# 49-CREAMY SHRIMP

**Preparation Time: 10 minutes**

**Cooking Time: 2 hours 10 minutes**

**Serves: 4**

**Ingredients:**

- 1 lb cooked shrimp
- 1 cup sour cream
- 10.5 oz can cream of mushroom soup
- 1 tsp curry powder
- 1 onion, chopped

**Directions:**

- Spray a medium pan with cooking spray and heat over medium heat.
- Add onion to the hot pan and sauté until onion is soft.
- Transfer sautéed onion to a crock pot along with the shrimp, curry powder, and cream of mushroom soup.
- Cover and cook on low for 2 hours.
- Stir in sour cream and serve.

**Nutritional Value (Amount per Serving):**

- Calories 302
- Fat 16.2 g
- Carbohydrates 9.5 g
- Sugar 1.8 g
- Protein 28.6 g
- Cholesterol 264 mg

# 50-Spicy Coconut Fish Stew

**Preparation Time: 10 minutes**

**Cooking Time: 6 hours 20 minutes**

**Serves: 6**

**Ingredients:**

- 1 ½ lb white fish fillets
- 14 oz coconut milk
- 14 oz can tomatoes, crushed
- 1 green bell pepper, chopped
- 1 red bell pepper, chopped
- 2 garlic cloves, minced
- 1 onion, chopped
- 1 Tbsp butter
- Pepper
- Salt

**Directions:**

- In a crock pot combine the butter, coconut milk, tomatoes, peppers, garlic, and onion.

- Cover and cook on low for 6 hours.
- A half hour before the time is up, open and add the fish fillets to the crock pot. Season with pepper and salt.
- Cover and cook on high for 30 minutes longer.
- Serve and enjoy.

**Nutritional Value (Amount per Serving):**

- Calories 398
- Fat 26.3 g
- Carbohydrates 11.6 g
- Sugar 6.9 g
- Protein 30.5 g
- Cholesterol 92 mg

# 51-ROSEMARY SALMON

**Preparation Time: 10 minutes**

**Cooking Time: 2 hours**

**Serves: 2**

**Ingredients:**

- 8 oz salmon
- 1/4 tsp fresh rosemary, minced
- 2 Tbsp fresh lemon juice
- 1/3 cup water
- 1 Tbsp capers
- 1 fresh lemon, sliced

**Directions:**

- Place salmon into a crock pot.
- Pour lemon juice and water over the salmon.
- Arrange lemon slices on top of the salmon.
- Sprinkle with rosemary and capers.
- Cover and cook on low for 2 hours.
- Serve and enjoy.

**Nutritional Value (Amount per Serving):**

- Calories 164
- Fat 7.3 g
- Carbohydrates 3.3 g
- Sugar 1.1 g
- Protein 22.6 g
- Cholesterol 50 mg

# 52-Paprika Garlic Shrimp

**Preparation Time: 10 minutes**

**Cooking Time: 50 minutes**

**Serves: 8**

**Ingredients:**

- 2 lb shrimp, peeled and deveined
- 1 tsp paprika
- 5 garlic cloves, sliced
- 3/4 cup olive oil
- 1/4 tsp red pepper flakes, crushed
- 1/4 tsp black pepper
- 1 tsp kosher salt

**Directions:**

- Combine oil, red pepper flakes, black pepper, paprika, garlic, and salt in a crock pot.
- Cover and cook on high for 30 minutes.
- Open and add the shrimp; cover and cook on high for 10 minutes.

- Open again and stir well. Cover and cook for 10 more minutes.
- Serve and enjoy.

**Nutritional Value (Amount per Serving):**

- Calories 301
- Fat 20.9 g
- Carbohydrates 2.6 g
- Sugar 0.1 g
- Protein 26 g
- Cholesterol 239 mg

# 53-Simple Lemon Halibut

**Preparation Time: 10 minutes**

**Cooking Time: 1 hour 30 minutes**

**Serves: 2**

**Ingredients:**

- 12 oz halibut fish fillet
- 1 Tbsp fresh lemon juice
- 1 Tbsp fresh dill
- 1 Tbsp olive oil
- Pepper
- Salt

**Directions:**

- Place fish fillet in the middle of a large sheet of aluminum foil. Season with pepper and salt.
- In a small bowl, whisk together dill, oil, and lemon juice. Pour over the fish fillet.
- Wrap foil around the fish fillet and make a packet.
- Place the foil packet in a crock pot.
- Cover and cook on high for 1 hour 30 minutes.

- Serve and enjoy.

**Nutritional Value (Amount per Serving):**

- Calories 289
- Fat 11.2 g
- Carbohydrates 1.1 g
- Sugar 0.2 g
- Protein 47 g
- Cholesterol 71 mg

# 54-CRAB DIP

**Preparation Time: 10 minutes**

**Cooking Time: 3 hours**

**Serves: 24**

**Ingredients:**

- 8 oz imitation crab meat
- 1 tsp paprika
- 2 Tbsp onion, chopped
- 8 oz cream cheese
- 1/4 cup walnuts, chopped
- 1 tsp hot sauce

**Directions:**

- Place all ingredients, except paprika and walnuts, in a crock pot and stir well.
- Sprinkle over the paprika and walnuts.
- Cover and cook on low for 3 hours.
- Stir well and serve.

**Nutritional Value (Amount per Serving):**

- Calories 53
- Fat 4.2 g
- Carbohydrates 2.4 g
- Sugar 0.6 g
- Protein 1.8 g
- Cholesterol 12 mg

# 55-Lemon Butter Tilapia

**Preparation Time: 10 minutes**

**Cooking Time: 2 hours**

**Serves: 4**

**Ingredients:**

- 4 tilapia fillets
- 1/4 tsp lemon pepper seasoning
- 3/4 cup fresh lemon juice
- 12 asparagus spear
- 2 Tbsp butter, divided

**Directions:**

- Prepare four large sheets of aluminum foil.
- Place a fish fillet on each sheet.
- Sprinkle lemon pepper seasoning and lemon juice on top of fish fillets.
- Add 1/2 tablespoon of butter on top of each fillet.
- Arrange three asparagus spears on each fish fillet.
- Fold foil around the fish fillet and make a packet.

- Repeat with the remaining fish fillets.
- Place fish fillet packets in a crock pot.
- Cover and cook on high for 2 hours.
- Serve and enjoy.

**Nutritional Value (Amount per Serving):**

- Calories 112
- Fat 6.7 g
- Carbohydrates 3.8 g
- Sugar 2.3 g
- Protein 10 g
- Cholesterol 37 mg

# SOUP, STEW AND CHILI RECIPES

## 56-Delicious Chicken Soup

**Preparation Time: 10 minutes**

**Cooking Time: 4 hours 30 minutes**

**Serves: 4**

**Ingredients:**

- 1 lb chicken breasts, boneless and skinless
- 2 Tbsp fresh basil, chopped
- 1 1/2 cups mozzarella cheese, shredded
- 2 garlic cloves, minced
- 1 Tbsp Parmesan cheese, grated
- 2 Tbsp dried basil
- 2 cups chicken stock
- 28 oz tomatoes, diced
- 1/4 tsp pepper
- 1/2 tsp salt

## Directions:

- Add chicken, Parmesan cheese, dried basil, tomatoes, garlic, pepper, and salt to a crock pot and stir well to combine.
- Cover and cook on low for 4 hours.
- Add fresh basil and mozzarella cheese and stir well.
- Cover again and cook for 30 more minutes or until cheese is melted.
- Remove chicken from the crock pot and shred using forks.
- Return shredded chicken to the crock pot and stir to mix.
- Serve and enjoy.

## Nutritional Value (Amount per Serving):

- Calories 299
- Fat 11.6 g
- Carbohydrates 9.3 g
- Sugar 5.6 g
- Protein 38.8 g
- Cholesterol 108 mg

# 57-Flavorful Broccoli Soup

**Preparation Time: 10 minutes**

**Cooking Time: 4 hours 15 minutes**

**Serves: 6**

**Ingredients:**

- 20 oz broccoli florets
- 4 oz cream cheese
- 8 oz cheddar cheese, shredded
- 1/2 tsp paprika
- 1/2 tsp ground mustard
- 3 cups chicken stock
- 2 garlic cloves, chopped
- 1 onion, diced
- 1 cup carrots, shredded
- 1/4 tsp baking soda
- 1/4 tsp salt

**Directions:**

- Add all ingredients except cream cheese and cheddar cheese to a crock pot and stir well.

- Cover and cook on low for 4 hours.
- Purée the soup using an immersion blender until smooth.
- Stir in the cream cheese and cheddar cheese.
- Cover and cook on low for 15 minutes longer.
- Season with pepper and salt.
- Serve and enjoy.

**Nutritional Value (Amount per Serving):**

- Calories 275
- Fat 19.9 g
- Carbohydrates 11.9 g
- Sugar 4 g
- Protein 14.4 g
- Cholesterol 60 mg

# 58-Healthy Chicken Kale Soup

**Preparation Time: 10 minutes**

**Cooking Time: 6 hours 15 minutes**

**Serves: 6**

**Ingredients:**

- 2 lb chicken breasts, skinless and boneless
- 1/4 cup fresh lemon juice
- 5 oz baby kale
- 32 oz chicken stock
- 1/2 cup olive oil
- 1 large onion, sliced
- 14 oz chicken broth
- 1 Tbsp extra-virgin olive oil
- Salt

**Directions:**

- Heat the extra-virgin olive oil in a pan over medium heat.
- Season chicken with salt and place in the hot pan.
- Cover pan and cook chicken for 15 minutes.

- Remove chicken from the pan and shred it using forks.
- Add shredded chicken to a crock pot.
- Add sliced onion, olive oil, and broth to a blender and blend until combined.
- Pour blended mixture into the crock pot.
- Add remaining ingredients to the crock pot and stir well.
- Cover and cook on low for 6 hours.
- Stir well and serve.

**Nutritional Value (Amount per Serving):**

- Calories 493
- Fat 31.3 g
- Carbohydrates 5.8 g
- Sugar 1.9 g
- Protein 46.7 g
- Cholesterol 135 mg

# 59-Spicy Chicken Pepper Stew

**Preparation Time: 10 minutes**

**Cooking Time: 6 hours**

**Serves: 6**

**Ingredients:**

- 3 chicken breasts, skinless and boneless, cut into small pieces
- 1 tsp garlic, minced
- 1 tsp ground ginger
- 2 tsp olive oil
- 2 tsp soy sauce
- 1 Tbsp fresh lemon juice
- 1/2 cup green onions, sliced
- 1 Tbsp crushed red pepper
- 8 oz chicken stock
- 1 bell pepper, chopped
- 1 green chili pepper, sliced
- 2 jalapeño peppers, sliced
- 1/2 tsp black pepper
- 1/4 tsp sea salt

## Directions:

- Add all ingredients to a large mixing bowl and mix well. Place in the refrigerator overnight.
- Pour marinated chicken mixture into a crock pot.
- Cover and cook on low for 6 hours.
- Stir well and serve.

## Nutritional Value (Amount per Serving):

- Calories 171
- Fat 7.4 g
- Carbohydrates 3.7 g
- Sugar 1.7 g
- Protein 22 g
- Cholesterol 65 mg

# 60-Beef Chili

**Preparation Time: 10 minutes**

**Cooking Time: 8 hours**

**Serves: 6**

**Ingredients:**

- 1 lb ground beef
- 1 tsp garlic powder
- 1 tsp paprika
- 3 tsp chili powder
- 1 Tbsp Worcestershire sauce
- 1 Tbsp fresh parsley, chopped
- 1 tsp onion powder
- 25 oz tomatoes, chopped
- 4 carrots, chopped
- 1 onion, diced
- 1 bell pepper, diced
- 1/2 tsp sea salt

**Directions:**

- Brown the ground meat in a pan over high heat until meat is no longer pink.
- Transfer meat to a crock pot.
- Add bell pepper, tomatoes, carrots, and onion to the crock pot and stir well.
- Add remaining ingredients and stir well.
- Cover and cook on low for 8 hours.
- Serve and enjoy.

**Nutritional Value (Amount per Serving):**

- Calories 152
- Fat 4 g
- Carbohydrates 10.4 g
- Sugar 5.8 g
- Protein 18.8 g
- Cholesterol 51 mg

# 61-TASTY BASIL TOMATO SOUP

**Preparation Time: 10 minutes**

**Cooking Time: 6 hours**

**Serves: 6**

**Ingredients:**

- 28 oz can whole peeled tomatoes
- 1/2 cup fresh basil leaves
- 4 cups chicken stock
- 1 tsp red pepper flakes
- 3 garlic cloves, peeled
- 2 onions, diced
- 3 carrots, peeled and diced
- 3 Tbsp olive oil
- 1 tsp salt

**Directions:**

- Add all ingredients to a crock pot and stir well.
- Cover and cook on low for 6 hours.
- Purée the soup until smooth using an immersion blender.

- Season soup with pepper and salt.
- Serve and enjoy.

**Nutritional Value (Amount per Serving):**

- Calories 126
- Fat 7.5 g
- Carbohydrates 13.3 g
- Sugar 7 g
- Protein 2.5 g
- Cholesterol 0 mg

# 62-HEALTHY SPINACH SOUP

**Preparation Time: 10 minutes**

**Cooking Time: 3 hours**

**Serves: 8**

**Ingredients:**

- 3 cups frozen spinach, chopped, thawed and drained
- 8 oz cheddar cheese, shredded
- 1 egg, lightly beaten
- 10 oz can cream of chicken soup
- 8 oz cream cheese, softened

**Directions:**

- Add spinach to a large bowl. Purée the spinach.
- Add egg, chicken soup, cream cheese, and pepper to the spinach purée and mix well.
- Transfer spinach mixture to a crock pot.
- Cover and cook on low for 3 hours.
- Stir in cheddar cheese and serve.

**Nutritional Value (Amount per Serving):**

- Calories 256
- Fat 21.9 g
- Carbohydrates 4.1 g
- Sugar 0.5 g
- Protein 11.1 g
- Cholesterol 84 mg

# 63-MEXICAN CHICKEN SOUP

**Preparation Time: 10 minutes**

**Cooking Time: 4 hours**

**Serves: 6**

**Ingredients:**

- 
- 1 1/2 lb chicken thighs, skinless and boneless
- 14 oz chicken stock
- 14 oz salsa
- 8 oz Monterey Jack cheese, shredded

**Directions:**

- Place chicken into a crock pot.
- Pour remaining ingredients over the chicken.
- Cover and cook on high for 4 hours.
- Remove chicken from crock pot and shred using forks.
- Return shredded chicken to the crock pot and stir well.
- Serve and enjoy.

**Nutritional Value (Amount per Serving):**

- Calories 371
- Fat 19.5 g
- Carbohydrates 5.7 g
- Sugar 2.2 g
- Protein 42.1 g
- Cholesterol 135 mg

# 64-Beef Stew

**Preparation Time: 10 minutes**

**Cooking Time: 5 hours 5 minutes**

**Serves: 8**

**Ingredients:**

- 3 lb beef stew meat, trimmed
- 1/2 cup red curry paste
- 1/3 cup tomato paste
- 13 oz can coconut milk
- 2 tsp ginger, minced
- 2 garlic cloves, minced
- 1 medium onion, sliced
- 2 Tbsp olive oil
- 2 cups carrots, julienned
- 2 cups broccoli florets
- 2 tsp fresh lime juice
- 2 Tbsp fish sauce
- 2 tsp sea salt

## Directions:

- Heat 1 tablespoon of oil in a pan over medium heat.
- Brown the meat on all sides in the pan.
- Add brown meat to a crock pot.
- Add remaining oil to the same pan and sauté the ginger, garlic, and onion over medium-high heat for 5 minutes.
- Add coconut milk and stir well.
- Transfer pan mixture to the crock pot.
- Add remaining ingredients except for carrots and broccoli.
- Cover and cook on high for 5 hours.
- Add carrots and broccoli during the last 30 minutes of cooking.
- Serve and enjoy.

## Nutritional Value (Amount per Serving):

- Calories 537
- Fat 28.6 g
- Carbohydrates 13 g
- Sugar 12.6 g
- Protein 54.4 g
- Cholesterol 152 mg

# 65-CREAMY BROCCOLI CAULIFLOWER SOUP

**Preparation Time: 10 minutes**

**Cooking Time: 6 hours**

**Serves: 6**

**Ingredients:**

- 2 cups cauliflower florets, chopped
- 3 cups broccoli florets, chopped
- 3 1/2 cups chicken stock
- 1 large carrot, diced
- 1/2 cup shallots, diced
- 2 garlic cloves, minced
- 1 cup plain yogurt
- 6 oz cheddar cheese, shredded
- 1 cup coconut milk
- Pepper
- Salt

**Directions:**

- Add all ingredients except milk, cheese, and yogurt to a crock pot and stir well.
- Cover and cook on low for 6 hours.

- Purée the soup using an immersion blender until smooth.
- Add cheese, milk, and yogurt and blend until smooth and creamy.
- Season with pepper and salt.
- Serve and enjoy.

**Nutritional Value (Amount per Serving):**

- Calories 281
- Fat 20 g
- Carbohydrates 14.4 g
- Sugar 6.9 g
- Protein 13.1 g
- Cholesterol 32 mg

# 66-SQUASH SOUP

**Preparation Time: 10 minutes**

**Cooking Time: 8 hours**

**Serves: 6**

**Ingredients:**

- 2 lb butternut squash, peeled, chopped into chunks
- 1 tsp ginger, minced
- 1/4 tsp cinnamon
- 1 Tbsp curry powder
- 2 bay leaves
- 1 tsp black pepper
- 1/2 cup heavy cream
- 2 cups chicken stock
- 1 Tbsp garlic, minced
- 2 carrots, cut into chunks
- 2 apples, peeled, cored and diced
- 1 large onion, diced
- 1 tsp salt

## Directions:

- Spray a crock pot inside with cooking spray.
- Add all ingredients except cream to the crock pot and stir well.
- Cover and cook on low for 8 hours.
- Purée the soup using an immersion blender until smooth and creamy.
- Stir in heavy cream and season soup with pepper and salt.
- Serve and enjoy.

## Nutritional Value (Amount per Serving):

- Calories 170
- Fat 4.4 g
- Carbohydrates 34.4 g
- Sugar 13.4g
- Protein 2.9 g
- Cholesterol 14 mg

# 67-Herb Tomato Soup

**Preparation Time: 10 minutes**

**Cooking Time: 6 hours**

**Serves: 8**

**Ingredients:**

- 55 oz can tomatoes, diced
- 1/2 onion, minced
- 2 cups chicken stock
- 1 cup half and half
- 4 Tbsp butter
- 1 bay leaf
- 1/2 tsp black pepper
- 1/2 tsp garlic powder
- 1 tsp oregano
- 1 tsp dried thyme
- 1 cup carrots, diced
- 1/4 tsp black pepper
- 1/2 tsp salt

**Directions:**

- Add all ingredients to a crock pot and stir well.
- Cover and cook on low for 6 hours.
- Discard bay leaf and purée the soup using an immersion blender until smooth.
- Serve and enjoy.

**Nutritional Value (Amount per Serving):**

- Calories 145
- Fat 9.4 g
- Carbohydrates 13.9 g
- Sugar 7.9 g
- Protein 3.2 g
- Cholesterol 26 mg

# 68-Easy Beef Mushroom Stew

**Preparation Time: 10 minutes**

**Cooking Time: 8 hours**

**Serves: 8**

**Ingredients:**

- 2 lb stewing beef, cubed
- 1 packet dry onion soup mix
- 4 oz can mushrooms, sliced
- 14 oz can cream of mushroom soup
- 1/2 cup water
- 1/4 tsp black pepper
- 1/2 tsp salt

**Directions:**

- Spray a crock pot inside with cooking spray.
- Add all ingredients into the crock pot and stir well.
- Cover and cook on low for 8 hours.
- Stir well and serve.

**Nutritional Value (Amount per Serving):**

- Calories 237
- Fat 8.5 g
- Carbohydrates 2.7 g
- Sugar 0.4 g
- Protein 35.1 g
- Cholesterol 101 mg

# 69-Lamb Stew

**Preparation Time: 10 minutes**

**Cooking Time: 8 hours**

**Serves: 2**

**Ingredients:**

- 1/2 lb lean lamb, boneless and cubed
- 2 Tbsp lemon juice
- 1/2 onion, chopped
- 2 garlic cloves, minced
- 2 fresh thyme sprigs
- 1/4 tsp turmeric
- 1/4 cup green olives, sliced
- 1/2 tsp black pepper
- 1/4 tsp salt

**Directions:**

- Add all ingredients to a crock pot and stir well.
- Cover and cook on low for 8 hours.
- Stir well and serve.

## Nutritional Value (Amount per Serving):

- Calories 297
- Fat 20.3 g
- Carbohydrates 5.4 g
- Sugar 1.5 g
- Protein 21 g
- Cholesterol 80 mg

# 70-Vegetable Chicken Soup

**Preparation Time: 10 minutes**

**Cooking Time: 6 hours**

**Serves: 6**

**Ingredients:**

- 4 cups chicken, boneless, skinless, cooked and diced
- 4 tsp garlic, minced
- 2/3 cups onion, diced
- 1 1/2 cups carrot, diced
- 6 cups chicken stock
- 2 Tbsp lime juice
- 1/4 cup jalapeño pepper, diced
- 1/2 cup tomatoes, diced
- 1/2 cup fresh cilantro, chopped
- 1 tsp chili powder
- 1 Tbsp cumin
- 1 3/4 cups tomato juice
- 2 tsp sea salt

**Directions:**

- Add all ingredients to a crock pot and stir well.
- Cover and cook on low for 6 hours.
- Stir well and serve.

**Nutritional Value (Amount per Serving):**

- Calories 192
- Fat 3.8 g
- Carbohydrates 9.8 g
- Sugar 5.7 g
- Protein 29.2 g
- Cholesterol 72 mg

# VEGETABLE AND SIDES RECIPES

## 71-SQUASH AND ZUCCHINI CASSEROLE

**Preparation Time: 10 minutes**

**Cooking Time: 6 hours**

**Serves: 6**

**Ingredients:**

- 2 cups yellow squash, quartered and sliced
- 2 cups zucchini, quartered and sliced
- 1/4 cup Parmesan cheese, grated
- 1/4 cup butter, cut into pieces
- 1 tsp garlic powder
- 1 tsp Italian seasoning
- 1/4 tsp pepper
- 1/2 tsp sea salt

**Directions:**

- Add sliced yellow squash and zucchini to a crock pot.
- Sprinkle with garlic powder, Italian seasoning, pepper, and salt.
- Top with grated cheese and butter.
- Cover with the lid and cook on low for 6 hours.
- Serve and enjoy.

**Nutritional Value (Amount per Serving):**

- Calories 107
- Fat 9.5 g
- Carbohydrates 2.5 g
- Sugar 1.3 g
- Protein 2.6 g
- Cholesterol 26 mg

# 72-Italian Zucchini

**Preparation Time: 10 minutes**

**Cooking Time: 3 hours**

**Serves: 3**

**Ingredients:**

- 2 zucchini, cut in half lengthwise then cut into half moons
- 1/4 cup Parmesan cheese, grated
- 1/2 tsp Italian seasoning
- 1 Tbsp olive oil
- 1 Tbsp butter
- 2 garlic cloves, minced
- 1 onion, sliced
- 2 tomatoes, diced
- 1/2 tsp pepper
- 1/4 tsp salt

**Directions:**

- Spray a crock pot inside with cooking spray.
- Add all ingredients except Parmesan cheese to the crock pot and stir well.

- Cover and cook on low for 3 hours.
- Top with the Parmesan cheese and serve.

**Nutritional Value (Amount per Serving):**

- Calories 181
- Fat 12.2 g
- Carbohydrates 12 g
- Sugar 6.1 g
- Protein 6.9 g
- Cholesterol 21 mg

# 73-Almond Green Beans

**Preparation Time: 10 minutes**

**Cooking Time: 3 hours**

**Serves: 4**

**Ingredients:**

- 1 lb green beans, rinsed and trimmed
- 1/2 cup almonds, sliced and toasted
- 1 cup vegetable stock
- 1/4 cup butter, melted
- 6 oz onion, sliced
- 1 Tbsp olive oil
- 1/4 tsp pepper
- 1/2 tsp salt

**Directions:**

- Heat the olive oil in a pan over medium heat.
- Add onion to the pan and sauté until softened.
- Transfer sautéed onion to a crock pot.
- Add remaining ingredients except for almonds to the crock pot and stir well.

- Cover and cook on low for 3 hours.
- Top with toasted almonds and serve.

**Nutritional Value (Amount per Serving):**

- Calories 253
- Fat 21.6 g
- Carbohydrates 14.5 g
- Sugar 4.1 g
- Protein 5.1 g
- Cholesterol 31 mg

# 74-Easy Ranch Mushrooms

**Preparation Time: 10 minutes**

**Cooking Time: 3 Hours**

**Serves: 6**

**Ingredients:**

- 2 lb mushrooms, rinsed, pat dry
- 2 packets ranch dressing mix
- 3/4 cup butter, melted
- 1/4 cup fresh parsley, chopped

**Directions:**

- Add all ingredients except parsley to a crock pot and stir well.
- Cover and cook on low for 3 hours.
- Garnish with parsley and serve.

**Nutritional Value (Amount per Serving):**

- Calories 237
- Fat 23.5 g

- Carbohydrates 5.2 g
- Sugar 2.6 g
- Protein 5.1 g
- Cholesterol 61 mg

# 75-Artichoke Spinach Dip

**Preparation Time: 10 minutes**

**Cooking Time: 6 hours**

**Serves: 6**

**Ingredients:**

- 8 oz cream cheese, softened
- 14 oz can artichoke hearts, drained and chopped
- 10 oz frozen spinach, thawed and drained
- 1/4 tsp garlic powder
- 2 Tbsp water
- 2 cups cottage cheese
- 1 tsp salt

**Directions:**

- Add spinach, cream cheese, cottage cheese, water, and artichoke hearts to a crock pot and stir well.
- Season with garlic powder and salt.
- Cover and cook on low for 6 hours.
- Stir well and serve.

**Nutritional Value (Amount per Serving):**

- Calories 230
- Fat 14.8 g
- Carbohydrates 8.9 g
- Sugar 1.1 g
- Protein 15.7 g
- Cholesterol 48 mg

# 76-Yummy Tomato Dip

**Preparation Time: 10 minutes**

**Cooking Time: 1 hour**

**Serves: 20**

**Ingredients:**

- 8 oz cream cheese
- 1/4 cup sun-dried tomatoes
- 1 Tbsp mayonnaise
- 3 garlic cloves
- 1/4 tsp white pepper
- 1 tsp pine nuts, toasted
- 3/4 oz fresh basil

**Directions:**

- Add all ingredients to a blender and blend until smooth.
- Pour mixture into a crock pot.
- Cover and cook on low for 1 hour.
- Stir well and serve.

**Nutritional Value (Amount per Serving):**

- Calories 47
- Fat 4.5 g
- Carbohydrates 1 g
- Sugar 0.1 g
- Protein 1 g
- Cholesterol 13 mg

# 77-CREAMY ONION DIP

**Preparation Time: 10 minutes**

**Cooking Time: 4 hours 30 minutes**

**Serves: 12**

**Ingredients:**

- 4 onions, sliced
- 2 Tbsp olive oil
- 2 Tbsp butter
- 1/2 cup mozzarella cheese
- 8 oz sour cream
- Pepper
- Salt

**Directions:**

- Add oil, butter, and onions to a crock pot.
- Cover and cook on high for 4 hours.
- Transfer onion mixture to a blender with the sour cream, pepper, and salt and blend until creamy.
- Return onion dip to the crock pot.

- Add mozzarella cheese and stir well. Cook on low for 30 minutes longer.
- Stir well and serve.

**Nutritional Value (Amount per Serving):**

- Calories 95
- Fat 8.5 g
- Carbohydrates 4.3 g
- Sugar 1.6 g
- Protein 1.4 g
- Cholesterol 14 mg

# 78-Italian Mushrooms

**Preparation Time: 10 minutes**

**Cooking Time: 4 hours**

**Serves: 6**

**Ingredients:**

- 1 lb mushrooms, cleaned
- 1 onion, sliced
- 1 packet Italian dressing mix
- 1/2 cup butter, melted

**Directions:**

- Add onion and mushrooms to a crock pot and mix well.
- Combine butter and Italian dressing mix and pour over the onion and mushrooms.
- Cover and cook on low for 4 hours.
- Serve and enjoy.

**Nutritional Value (Amount per Serving):**

- Calories 162
- Fat 15.6 g
- Carbohydrates 4.8 g
- Sugar 2.4 g
- Protein 2.8 g
- Cholesterol 41 mg

# 79-Garlic Cheese Spinach

**Preparation Time: 10 minutes**

**Cooking Time: 1 hour**

**Serves: 4**

**Ingredients:**

- 16 oz baby spinach
- 2 garlic cloves, minced
- 1 cup cheddar cheese, shredded
- 3 oz cream cheese

**Directions:**

- Add all ingredients to a crock pot and stir well.
- Cover and cook on high for 1 hour.
- Stir well and serve.

**Nutritional Value (Amount per Serving):**

- Calories 216
- Fat 17.2 g

- Carbohydrates 5.6 g
- Sugar 0.7 g
- Protein 12 g
- Cholesterol 53 mg

# 80-SIMPLE DILL CARROTS

**Preparation Time: 10 minutes**

**Cooking Time: 2 hours**

**Serves: 6**

**Ingredients:**

- 1 lb carrots, peeled and cut into round pieces on the diagonal
- 1 Tbsp butter
- 1 Tbsp fresh dill, minced
- 3 Tbsp water

**Directions:**

- Add all ingredients to a crock pot and stir well.
- Cover and cook on low for 2 hours.
- Stir well and serve.

**Nutritional Value (Amount per Serving):**

- Calories 49
- Fat 1.9 g

- Carbohydrates 7.7 g
- Sugar 3.7 g
- Protein 0.7 g
- Cholesterol 5 mg

# 81-ROSEMARY GREEN BEANS

**Preparation Time: 10 minutes**

**Cooking Time: 1 hour 30 minutes**

**Serves: 4**

**Ingredients:**

- 1 lb green beans, washed and trimmed
- 2 Tbsp fresh lemon juice
- 1 tsp fresh thyme, minced
- 2 Tbsp water
- 1 Tbsp fresh rosemary, minced

**Directions:**

- Add all ingredients to a crock pot and stir well.
- Cover and cook on low for 1 1/2 hours.
- Stir well and serve.

**Nutritional Value (Amount per Serving):**

- Calories 40
- Fat 0.4 g
- Carbohydrates 8.9 g

- Sugar 1.8 g
- Protein 2.2 g
- Cholesterol 0 mg

# 82-Vegetable Stew

**Preparation Time: 10 minutes**

**Cooking Time: 2 hours**

**Serves: 12**

**Ingredients:**

- 3 cups carrots, shredded
- 32 oz vegetable stock
- 1 cup cilantro, chopped
- 2 jalapeños, chopped
- 5 garlic cloves, minced
- 2 cups water
- 1 Tbsp cumin
- 1 Tbsp chili powder
- 2 Tbsp tomato paste
- 4 tomatoes, diced
- 1 large onion, diced
- 2 zucchini, chopped
- 1/2 head cabbage, chopped
- Pepper
- Salt

## Directions:

- Add all ingredients to a crock pot and stir well.
- Cover and cook on low for 2 hours.
- Stir well and serve.

## Nutritional Value (Amount per Serving):

- Calories 57
- Fat 0.9 g
- Carbohydrates 10.2 g
- Sugar 5.5 g
- Protein 3.5 g
- Cholesterol 0 mg

# 83-Tasty Vegetable Fajitas

**Preparation Time: 10 minutes**

**Cooking Time: 3 hours 30 minutes**

**Serves: 4**

**Ingredients:**

- 1 cup cherry tomatoes, halved
- 3 bell peppers, cut into strips
- 1 onion, sliced
- 1 tsp paprika
- 1 Tbsp olive oil
- Pepper and salt

**Directions:**

- Add onion, bell peppers, oil, smoked paprika, pepper, and salt to a crock pot and stir well.
- Cover and cook on high for 1 1/2 hours.
- Add cherry tomatoes and cook for 2 hours longer.
- Stir well and serve.

**Nutritional Value (Amount per Serving):**

- Calories 79
- Fat 3.9 g
- Carbohydrates 11.4 g
- Sugar 6.9 g
- Protein 1.7 g
- Cholesterol 0 mg

# 84-SIMPLE ROASTED BROCCOLI

**Preparation Time: 10 minutes**

**Cooking Time: 2 hours**

**Serves: 4**

**Ingredients:**

- 2 lb broccoli florets
- 1 bell pepper, chopped
- 2 tsp olive oil
- Pepper and salt

**Directions:**

- Add all ingredients to a crock pot and stir well to mix.
- Cover and cook on high for 2 hours.
- Stir well and serve.

**Nutritional Value (Amount per Serving):**

- Calories 89
- Fat 3.2 g
- Carbohydrates 13.3 g

- Sugar 0.7 g
- Protein 7 g
- Cholesterol 0 mg

# 85-TOMATOES, GARLIC AND OKRA

**Preparation Time: 10 minutes**

**Cooking Time: 2 hours**

**Serves: 4**

**Ingredients:**

- 1 1/2 cups okra, diced
- 1 small onion, diced
- 2 large tomatoes, diced
- 1 tsp hot sauce
- 2 garlic cloves, minced

**Directions:**

- Add all ingredients to a crock pot and stir well.
- Cover and cook on low for 2 hours.
- Stir well and serve.

**Nutritional Value (Amount per Serving):**

- Calories 41
- Fat 0.3 g
- Carbohydrates 8.5 g
- Sugar 3.7 g

- Protein 1.8 g
- Cholesterol 0 mg

# DESSERT RECIPES

## 86-Delicious Pumpkin Custard

**Preparation Time: 10 minutes**

**Cooking Time: 2 hours 30 minutes**

**Serves: 6**

**Ingredients:**

- 4 large eggs
- 4 Tbsp coconut oil, melted
- 1 tsp pumpkin pie spice
- 1/2 cup almond flour
- 1 tsp vanilla
- 1 cup pumpkin purée
- 1/2 cup erythritol
- Pinch of salt

**Directions:**

- Spray the inside of a crock pot with cooking spray.

- Add eggs to a large mixing bowl and blend until smooth using a hand mixer. Slowly beat in the sweetener.
- Add vanilla and pumpkin purée to the egg mixture and blend well.
- Add almond flour, pumpkin pie spice, salt, and coconut oil and blend until well combined.
- Pour mixture into the crock pot.
- Place a paper towel on the crock pot and cover.
- Cook on low for 2 hours 30 minutes.
- Cut into servings, serve and enjoy.

**Nutritional Value (Amount per Serving):**

- Calories 196
- Fat 17.2 g
- Carbohydrates 5.8 g
- Sugar 2.1 g
- Protein 6.7 g
- Cholesterol 124 mg

# 87-LEMON BLUEBERRY CAKE

**Preparation Time: 10 minutes**

**Cooking Time: 3 hours**

**Serves: 12**

**Ingredients:**

- 6 eggs, separated
- ½ cup fresh blueberries
- 2 cups heavy cream
- 1/2 cup Swerve
- 1/3 cup fresh lemon juice
- 1 tsp lemon zest
- 1/2 cup coconut flour
- 1/2 tsp salt

**Directions:**

- Add egg whites to a large mixing bowl and beat until stiff peaks form. Set aside.
- In another bowl, whisk egg yolks with heavy cream, Swerve, lemon juice, lemon zest, coconut flour, and salt.

- Slowly fold the egg whites into the egg yolk mixture until well combined.
- Spray the inside of a crock pot with cooking spray.
- Pour prepared batter into the crock pot.
- Sprinkle blueberries on top of batter.
- Cover and cook on low for 3 hours.
- Allow to cool completely, cut and serve.

**Nutritional Value (Amount per Serving):**

- Calories 108
- Fat 9.7 g
- Carbohydrates 2.2 g
- Sugar 1 g
- Protein 3.4 g
- Cholesterol 109 mg

# 88-Tasty Lemon Cake

**Preparation Time: 10 minutes**

**Cooking Time: 3 hours**

**Serves: 8**

**Ingredients:**

- 2 eggs
- Zest of 1 lemon
- 1 Tbsp lemon juice
- 1/2 cup whipping cream
- 1/2 cup butter, melted
- 2 tsp baking powder
- 6 Tbsp Swerve
- 1/2 cup coconut flour
- 1 1/2 cups almond flour
- For topping:
- 2 Tbsp fresh lemon juice
- 2 Tbsp butter, melted
- 1/2 cup hot water
- 3 Tbsp Swerve

**Directions:**

- In a mixing bowl, mix together almond flour, baking powder, Swerve, and coconut flour.
- In a large bowl, whisk together eggs, lemon zest, 1 tablespoon lemon juice, butter, and whipping cream.
- Add almond flour mixture to the egg mixture and stir until well combined.
- Spray the inside of a crock pot with cooking spray.
- Pour batter into the crock pot and spread well.
- In a bowl, combine together all topping ingredients and pour over the cake batter.
- Cover and cook on high for 3 hours.
- Serve warm cut into squares and enjoy.

**Nutritional Value (Amount per Serving):**

- Calories 294
- Fat 28.5 g
- Carbohydrates 7.4 g
- Sugar 0.9 g
- Protein 6.3 g
- Cholesterol 87 mg

# 89-CHOCOLATE CAKE

**Preparation Time: 10 minutes**

**Cooking Time: 2 hours 30 minutes**

**Serves: 10**

**Ingredients:**

- 3 large eggs
- 1/2 tsp vanilla
- 2/3 cup unsweetened almond milk
- 6 Tbsp butter, melted
- 1 1/2 tsp baking powder
- 3 Tbsp whey protein powder
- 1/2 cup unsweetened cocoa powder
- 1/2 cup Swerve
- 1 cup almond flour
- Pinch of salt

**Directions:**

- Spray a crock pot inside with cooking spray.
- In a mixing bowl, whisk together almond flour, baking powder, protein powder, cocoa powder, Swerve, and salt.

- Stir in eggs, vanilla, almond milk, and butter until well combined.
- Pour batter into the crock pot.
- Cover and cook on low for 2 1/2 hours.
- Serve warm cut into squares and enjoy.

**Nutritional Value (Amount per Serving):**

- Calories 176
- Fat 15 g
- Carbohydrates 6.3 g
- Sugar 0.8 g
- Protein 7.9 g
- Cholesterol 79 mg

# 90-COCONUT RASPBERRY CAKE

**Preparation Time: 10 minutes**

**Cooking Time: 3 hours**

**Serves: 10**

**Ingredients:**

- 4 large eggs
- 1 cup raspberries
- 1 tsp vanilla
- 3/4 cup unsweetened coconut milk
- 1/2 cup coconut oil, melted
- 2 tsp baking soda
- 1/4 cup powdered egg whites
- 3/4 cup Swerve
- 1 cup unsweetened shredded coconut
- 2 cups almond flour
- Pinch of salt

**Directions:**

- Spray a crock pot inside with cooking spray.

- In a mixing bowl, whisk together almond flour, baking soda, powdered egg whites, Swerve, shredded coconut, and salt.
- Stir in eggs, vanilla, coconut milk, and coconut oil until well combined.
- Add raspberries and fold well.
- Pour batter into the crock pot and spread well.
- Cover and cook on low for 3 hours.
- Slice, serve and enjoy.

**Nutritional Value (Amount per Serving):**

- Calories 382
- Fat 34.9 g
- Carbohydrates 10.1 g
- Sugar 3.1 g
- Protein 10.9 g
- Cholesterol 74 mg

# 91-CHOCOLATE FUDGE

**Preparation Time: 10 minutes**

**Cooking Time: 2 hours**

**Serves: 30**

**Ingredients:**

- 2 1/2 cups unsweetened chocolate chips
- 1 tsp vanilla
- 1/3 cup unsweetened coconut milk
- Pinch of salt

**Directions:**

- Add all ingredients to a crock pot and stir well.
- Cover and cook on low for 2 hours.
- Stir until smooth. Line a baking dish with parchment paper.
- Spread fudge mixture in prepared baking dish and place in the refrigerator for 30 minutes.
- Serve chilled, cut into squares and enjoy.

**Nutritional Value (Amount per Serving):**

- Calories 134
- Fat 10.7 g
- Carbohydrates 5.4 g
- Sugar 0 g
- Protein 2.7 g
- Cholesterol 0 mg

# 92-YUMMY BROWNIE BITES

**Preparation Time: 10 minutes**

**Cooking Time: 4 hours**

**Serves: 10**

**Ingredients:**

- 2 eggs
- 2 cups almond flour
- 1/3 cup water
- 1 tsp vanilla
- 1/2 cup coconut oil, melted
- 1/2 cup unsweetened coconut milk
- 2 tsp baking soda
- 2 tsp baking powder
- 3/4 cup cocoa powder
- 1 cup Swerve
- Pinch of salt

**Directions:**

- Spray a crock pot inside with cooking spray.

- In a large bowl, mix together all ingredients and pour into the crock pot and spread well.
- Cover and cook on low for 4 hours.
- Allow brownie mixture to cool for 30 minutes. Scoop out brownie mixture with an ice cream scoop and form into balls.
- Serve and enjoy.

**Nutritional Value (Amount per Serving):**

- Calories 279
- Fat 26.7 g
- Carbohydrates 9.8 g
- Sugar 1.4 g
- Protein 7.4 g
- Cholesterol 33 mg

# 93-MOIST BERRY CAKE

**Preparation Time: 10 minutes**

**Cooking Time: 3 hours**

**Serves: 10**

**Ingredients:**

- 4 eggs
- 2 tsp baking soda
- 1/4 cup protein powder
- 1/2 cup Swerve
- 1 cup unsweetened shredded coconut
- 2 cups almond flour
- 1/3 cup unsweetened chocolate chips
- 1 cup blackberries
- 1/2 cup heavy cream
- 1/4 cup butter, melted
- 1/4 cup coconut oil, melted
- Pinch of salt

## Directions:

- Spray a crock pot inside with cooking spray.
- In a large bowl, mix together almond flour, baking soda, protein powder, Swerve, coconut, and salt.
- Stir in heavy cream, butter, coconut oil, and eggs until combined.
- Add chocolate chips and blackberries and fold well.
- Pour batter into the crock pot and spread evenly.
- Cover and cook on low for 3 hours.
- Allow to cool completely and serve.

## Nutritional Value (Amount per Serving):

- Calories 382
- Fat 32.3 g
- Carbohydrates 9.9 g
- Sugar 2.1 g
- Protein 16.7 g
- Cholesterol 86 mg

# 94-Chocó Almond Fudge

**Preparation Time: 10 minutes**

**Cooking Time: 6 hours**

**Serves: 30**

**Ingredients:**

- 2 Tbsp almonds, sliced
- 2 Tbsp Swerve
- 8 oz unsweetened chocolate chips
- 1/2 cup unsweetened coconut milk
- 1 Tbsp butter, melted

**Directions:**

- Grease an 8-inch baking dish with butter and set aside.
- Add chocolate chips, coconut milk, butter, and Swerve to a crock pot and mix well.
- Cover the crock pot with the lid and cook on low for 2 hours.
- Add almonds and stir fudge until smooth.
- Pour fudge mixture into a baking dish and spread evenly. Place in the refrigerator for 6 hours.
- Cut into squares and serve.

**Nutritional Value (Amount per Serving):**

- Calories 66
- Fat 5.6 g
- Carbohydrates 2.5 g
- Sugar 0.2 g
- Protein 1.2 g
- Cholesterol 1 mg

# 95-DELICIOUS PUMPKIN CUSTARD

**Preparation Time: 10 minutes**

**Cooking Time: 5 hours**

**Serves: 6**

**Ingredients:**

- 6 eggs
- 3 cups canned pumpkin purée
- 2 Tbsp coconut oil
- 10 drops liquid Stevia
- 1/4 cup unsweetened coconut milk

**Directions:**

- Pour 1 inch of water into a crock pot.
- Add all ingredients to a blender and blend until smooth.
- Spray six ramekins with cooking spray.
- Pour blended mixture into the prepared ramekins and place into the crock pot.
- Cover and cook on high for 5 hours.
- Serve warm and enjoy.

**Nutritional Value (Amount per Serving):**

- Calories 146
- Fat 11.3 g
- Carbohydrates 5.9 g
- Sugar 2.7 g
- Protein 6.3 g
- Cholesterol 164 mg

# BROTHS, STOCKS AND SAUCES

## 96-MIXED BERRY SAUCE

**Preparation Time: 10 minutes**

**Cooking Time: 3 hours**

**Serves: 8**

**Ingredients:**

- 4 oz fresh blueberries
- 6 oz fresh blackberries
- 8 oz fresh strawberries
- 1/4 cup erythritol

**Directions:**

- Add all ingredients to a crock pot and stir well.
- Cover and cook on low for 3 hours.
- Allow to cool completely and store in an air-tight container.

**Nutritional Value (Amount per Serving):**

- Calories 26
- Fat 0.2 g
- Carbohydrates 6.3 g
- Sugar 3.8 g
- Protein 0.6 g
- Cholesterol 0 mg

# 97-APPLE CRANBERRY SAUCE

**Preparation Time: 10 minutes**

**Cooking Time: 2 hours**

**Serves: 16**

**Ingredients:**

- 3 cups fresh cranberries
- 1/2 tsp cinnamon
- 1 Tbsp honey
- 1/2 fresh lime juice
- 1/4 cup fresh orange juice
- 1 apple, cored ,peeled and diced
- 10 strawberries
- 1 cup dried cranberries
- 1/4 tsp salt

**Directions:**

- Add all ingredients to a crock pot and stir well.
- Cover and cook on high for 2 hours.
- Purée the sauce using an immersion blender.

- Allow to cool completely and store in an air-tight container.

**Nutritional Value (Amount per Serving):**

- Calories 60
- Fat 0.1 g
- Carbohydrates 14 g
- Sugar 11.8 g
- Protein 0.1 g
- Cholesterol 0 mg

# 98-Fresh Cranberry Sauce

**Preparation Time: 10 minutes**

**Cooking Time: 3 hours**

**Serves: 8**

**Ingredients:**

- 12 oz fresh cranberries, rinsed
- 1 tsp ginger, grated
- 1 tsp orange zest
- 1/2 cup water
- 1/2 cup orange juice

**Directions:**

- Add all ingredients to a crock pot and stir well.
- Cover and cook on low for 3 hours.
- Gently mash the cranberries using a spoon until you have the desired consistency.

**Nutritional Value (Amount per Serving):**

- Calories 31
- Fat 0 g
- Carbohydrates 5.7 g

- Sugar 2.9 g
- Protein 0.1 g
- Cholesterol 0 mg

# 99-BONE BROTH

**Preparation Time: 10 minutes**

**Cooking Time: 24 hours**

**Serves: 4**

**Ingredients:**

- 5 lb beef bones
- 4 parsley sprigs
- 2 Tbsp peppercorns
- 2 bay leaves
- 2 celery stalks
- 2 carrots, peeled and cut in half
- 2 onions, quartered
- 2 Tbsp apple cider vinegar
- 1 tsp kosher salt

**Directions:**

- Add beef bones to a crock pot and place remaining ingredients on top of the bones.
- Pour enough water into the crock pot to cover everything.

- Cover and cook on high for 24 hours.
- Strain the liquid into a container and store in the refrigerator.

**Nutritional Value (Amount per Serving):**

- Calories 45
- Fat 0.2 g
- Carbohydrates 10.5 g
- Sugar 4 g
- Protein 1.3 g
- Cholesterol 0 mg

# 100-TURKEY STOCK

**Preparation Time: 10 minutes**

**Cooking Time: 24 hours**

**Serves: 10**

**Ingredients:**

- 1 whole turkey
- 1 Tbsp whole peppercorns
- 1 onion, cut in half
- 2 celery stalks, chopped
- 1 carrot, chopped
- Water

**Directions:**

- Place turkey in a crock pot.
- Add peppercorns and vegetables on top of the turkey.
- Fill crock pot with water.
- Cover and cook on low for 24 hours.
- Strain the stock into a container and store in the refrigerator.

**Nutritional Value (Amount per Serving):**

- Calories 10
- Fat 0 g
- Carbohydrates 2 g
- Sugar 1 g
- Protein 0 g
- Cholesterol 0 mg

# 101-APPLESAUCE

**Preparation Time: 10 minutes**

**Cooking Time: 2 hours**

**Serves: 6**

**Ingredients:**

- 3 lb apples, peeled, cored, and sliced
- 2 cinnamon sticks
- 2 Tbsp fresh lemon juice
- 1/4 cup water

**Directions:**

- Add all ingredients to a crock pot and stir well.
- Cover and cook on high for 2 hours.
- Discard cinnamon sticks and mash the apples with a potato masher until you have the desired consistency.

**Nutritional Value (Amount per Serving):**

- Calories 59
- Fat 0.2 g

- Carbohydrates 15 g
- Sugar 11.7 g
- Protein 0.3 g
- Cholesterol 0 mg

# 102-Peach Sauce

**Preparation Time: 10 minutes**

**Cooking Time: 8 hours**

**Serves: 6**

**Ingredients:**

- 4 lb frozen peaches, thawed
- 1/4 tsp ground cloves
- 1/2 tsp ground ginger
- 1 tsp fresh lemon juice
- 1/2 cup Swerve

**Directions:**

- Add peaches to a blender and blend until smooth and creamy.
- Transfer blended peaches to a crock pot along with Swerve and stir well.
- Cover and cook on low for 8 hours.
- Stir in cloves, ginger, and lemon juice.
- Allow to cool completely and store in a container in the refrigerator.

## Nutritional Value (Amount per Serving):

- Calories 41
- Fat 0.3 g
- Carbohydrates 9.7 g
- Sugar 9.4 g
- Protein 1 g
- Cholesterol 0 mg

# 103-Ham Stock

**Preparation Time: 10 minutes**

**Cooking Time: 24 hours**

**Serves: 14**

**Ingredients:**

- 1 large ham bone
- 1 tsp black peppercorns
- 1 bay leaf
- 1 thyme sprig
- 1 garlic clove, peeled
- 2 carrots, cut in half
- 1 celery stalk, cut in half
- 1 onion, peeled and quartered

**Directions:**

- Add all ingredients to a crock pot.
- Fill crock pot with cold water.
- Cover and cook on low for 24 hours.

- Strain the stock into a container and store in the refrigerator.

**Nutritional Value (Amount per Serving):**

- Calories 10
- Fat 0 g
- Carbohydrates 2 g
- Sugar 1 g
- Protein 0 g
- Cholesterol 0 mg

# 104-Delicious Strawberry Sauce

**Preparation Time: 10 minutes**

**Cooking Time: 2 hours**

**Serves: 4**

**Ingredients:**

- 1 lb strawberries, hulled and chopped
- 1 Tbsp fresh lemon juice
- 1/4 cup Swerve
- Pinch of salt

**Directions:**

- Add strawberries, Swerve, and salt to a crock pot.
- Cover and cook on low for 2 hours.
- Add lemon juice and stir well.
- Once sauce has cooled completely, pour it into a container and store in the refrigerator.

**Nutritional Value (Amount per Serving):**

- Calories 38

- Fat 0.4 g
- Carbohydrates 8.9 g
- Sugar 5.6 g
- Protein 0.8 g
- Cholesterol 0 mg

# 105-BLUEBERRY APPLE SAUCE

**Preparation Time: 10 minutes**

**Cooking Time: 4 hours**

**Serves: 4**

**Ingredients:**

- 1 1/2 lb apples
- 1 tsp cinnamon
- 2 Tbsp water
- 4 oz blueberries

**Directions:**

- Add all ingredients to a crock pot and stir to mix.
- Cover and cook on low for 4 hours.
- Blend the sauce using an immersion blender until the desired consistency.
- Once sauce has cooled completely, store in a container in the refrigerator.

**Nutritional Value (Amount per Serving):**

- Calories 61
- Fat 0.3 g
- Carbohydrates 16.1 g
- Sugar 11.5 g
- Protein 0.5 g
- Cholesterol 0 mg

# CONCLUSION

A low-carb diet is one of the healthiest diets for a healthy lifestyle and healthy weight loss plan. It is rich in vegetables, fruits, and lean meat. In this low-carb crock pot cookbook you will find a huge collection of healthy, delicious and nutritious recipes.

Everyone from the beginner to the experienced cook can make these easy recipes. Just choose your favorite recipe and start cooking!

Made in the USA
Monee, IL
26 September 2020

43398541R00125